My Life with Women

RICHARD ARMOUR

My Life
with
Women

Confessions of a Domesticated Male

Illustrated by Leo Hershfield

McGraw-Hill Book Company

NEW YORK   TORONTO   LONDON   SYDNEY

My Life with Women
Confessions of a Domesticated Male

Library of Congress Catalog Card Number: 67-22950

Second Printing—November, 1968

Dedicated to Kathleen,

my loving wife, who after reading

this book is still my loving wife.

Acknowledgments

Most of the verses first appeared in *Family Weekly, Good Housekeeping, Look, Los Angeles Times, McCall's, Quote, The Saturday Evening Post, The Wall Street Journal,* and *Westways.* Chapter X was published in *Woman's Day,* and chapters XI, XIII, and XV were adapted from articles in the *Orange County Sun.* I am grateful for permission to reprint this material.

One

Until I was eight years old, I had no thought of getting married. Though small for my age, I was the best marble player in our block, with a large bag of aggies and immies that I had won while playing for keeps. My mind was on marbles, not women, and there seemed no reason for any change, especially when I was doing so well.

It is not that I was unaware of sex, or at least of the difference between the sexes. There was a blonde next door who was seven and a half, going on eight, and she was always coming over to our house and hanging around. I knew what she was after: my marbles. Once, to get rid of her, I gave her a couple of dobies, but that must have given her the idea she was making progress and might get some aggies out of me if she kept at it.

But that's all she ever got, just those dobies. I might have given her more, if I had liked her, but I didn't. She was too fat. And she picked her nose.

However, it was from this girl next door, the first

blonde in my life, that I learned about the difference between the sexes. It was very simple. Boys can play marbles and girls can't. This girl used to beg me to show her how, and I did, but she could never learn. There was something wrong with her aim, or she didn't have any muscle in her thumb, or something.

One day I let her have it. "The trouble with you," I told her, "is that you are a girl."

This hit her pretty hard. For a while she just stood there, picking her nose. Then she started bawling and ran home.

The sad part about it was that after she had had a good cry, and her mother had washed her face, which really needed it, she came back over to our house as if nothing had happened. The way I disliked that girl, it's a wonder I wasn't finished with women for life. Certainly she contributed to my decision, when I was eight years old, never to marry.

Then I fell in love with Miss Webster, and everything changed.

Miss Webster was my third-grade teacher and all I had ever hoped for in a woman. She had a soft, sweet voice. Her eyes crinkled when she smiled. She smelled good. And she could write on the board without making the chalk squeak.

One day when I came home from school, I broke the news to my mother, who was in the kitchen making cookies.

"I'm going to marry Miss Webster," I said.

"That's nice," my mother said, not the least surprised. It was almost as if she already knew. Could Miss Webster have told her? And yet I hadn't told Miss Webster myself.

"And we're going to have two children, both boys," I said.

"That's fine," my mother said. "Now you can scrape the bowl and lick the spoon."

All the time I was scraping the bowl and licking the spoon, I was thinking of Miss Webster. We were going to be very happy together. I would look after her and give her everything she wanted, and she could just stay home and make cookies.

A short time afterward, I disclosed my plans to one of my friends during recess while we were swinging on the monkey bars.

"I'm going to marry Miss Webster," I said.

"So am I," he said.

This came as a surprise to me. I was even more surprised to learn, after a little asking around, that every boy in the class planned to marry Miss Webster. I was not greatly disturbed, however, since I had an advantage over most of the others. We were seated alphabetically, and I sat in the front row. I was much closer to Miss Webster than boys like Jack Williams and Eddy Zorn. Besides, Miss Webster obviously liked me. Who else got to clap erasers twice a week?

But I had competition more serious than my

[3]

classmates. One day I saw Miss Webster go by in a sporty car with the top down. She smiled and waved at me. I waved back but I couldn't smile. A man was driving the car, and he had one hand on the steering wheel and the other around Miss Webster. After waving at me, Miss Webster said something to the man, and he turned and looked back at me and laughed.

As the car drove on and disappeared around a corner, I had a feeling that I was losing Miss Webster. For the first time it occurred to me that she might marry someone else, someone who owned a car and was old enough to drive it.

I was right about Miss Webster. Just before the end of the school year, when I should have been excited about summer vacation and being promoted to fourth grade, I got the bad news. Though I had rather expected it, I was pretty depressed for several days.

"I am not going to teach after this year," Miss Webster told our class. "I am getting married." The girls cried, they were so happy, and the boys would have cried too, if they had not been boys. As it was, they just looked miserable.

It was the first time I had ever been beaten out by a rival, and I took it hard. Miss Webster had led me on and then let me down. But she wasn't as much to blame as the man in the car. I hated him. A couple of times I imagined myself fighting a duel with him, the winner to get Miss Webster. One time it was with swords and one time it was with pistols, and I won both times. But I couldn't go on imagining forever, and when I wasn't imagining I knew I had lost Miss Webster for good.

When I came home from school and told my mother Miss Webster was getting married, she sympathized with me.

"I know how you feel," she said. "But I've always thought she was a little old for you."

Then she told me that Miss Webster was twenty-two, and by the time I was twenty-two she would be thirty-six. By the time I was thirty-six she would be fifty.

"A woman can be older than her husband," she said, "but she shouldn't be too much older. I'm three years older than your father, and that's about enough."

"Why?" I asked.

"Well, it just is," she said, and seemed to think this a satisfactory answer. It was all I could get out of her.

By the time I was eight years old, I had learned a good deal about women. From the girl next door I learned that the ones who are always after you are the ones you don't want. From Miss Webster I learned that the ones you want are always the wrong age or something, and then somebody comes and carries them off anyhow.

It was discouraging enough to lose Miss Webster, but that wasn't all. A boy moved into the neighborhood who could knuckle better than I could, and he won all of my aggies and most of my immies.

It was a bad year for me.

After that unfortunate experience with Miss Webster, I thought I was through with women. This was only partly because I had been beaten out by a rival suitor. It was also because, about the same time, I was given a bicycle by my parents, who thought I needed cheering up. I got so busy riding that bicycle and oiling it and polishing it that for a while I forgot about women entirely. You just can't think about women when you are pedaling hard and ringing your bell and being chased by a dog.

But this didn't last long. I was barely nine when

Carl Hawkins, who was ten and big for his age, told me some things about Lucille Briggs, who was also ten and big for her age (they were all big for their age but me), that started me thinking. My first reaction was disbelief.

"You're making it up," I said to Carl.

"No, I'm not," Carl said. "Cross my heart."

According to Carl, Lucille had come over to his house one morning when she knew his mother and father were away, and she had done some really peculiar things. She had done them in a clothes closet into which she had taken Carl after locking the closet door. It was hot and stuffy in there and the light wasn't any too good, but Carl swore he could see perfectly well and this was the way it was.

I asked Carl to tell me the whole thing over again because I wasn't sure I had got it straight, and he did, gladly.

Well, I was really amazed. Momentarily, I forgot about my bicycle. I kept thinking about Lucille, in that closet with the door locked. I wondered what I would do if Lucille, who lived in the middle of the next block, ever came down to my house and did these things.

Once, when my parents were away, Lucille came over to our house and I fully expected her to head straight for our hall closet and pull me in there with her and lock the door. I was frightened and confused, and I tried to remember everything Carl had told me. But Lucille only wanted to get a bowl her mother had lent my mother. She went out to the kitchen, right past the closet, and came back to the front door, past the closet again, and all she said to me was, "My mother said that if your mother kept the bowl much longer she'd think she owned it."

When Lucille left, carrying the bowl, I was relieved and disappointed, about half and half. After all, I was only nine and she was ten. Besides, as I have said, I was small for my age. I was lucky I had an older friend like Carl, who would tell me everything.

For the next couple of years, Carl kept me posted. As soon as he learned anything, he let me know. For instance, he got hold of a book called *How Babies Are Born,* and we went over to his garage and climbed up a ladder into a storage place and put the book on top of an old trunk and turned the pages. We especially studied the drawings, which were easier to understand than the writing.

"I see now," I said. "I could never quite figure it out before."

"I've been trying to tell you," Carl said. "I've known about it ever since that time Lucille came over to our house."

Carl was twelve now, and according to the book he was old enough to become a father. Just thinking about it made him feel pretty important. As for me, I had a year to go.

Two

I was barely twelve when Carl moved away and I was left on my own. We had one final session out in his garage.

"Is there anything else you need to know?" he asked me. He was smoking a cigarette and looking very worldly.

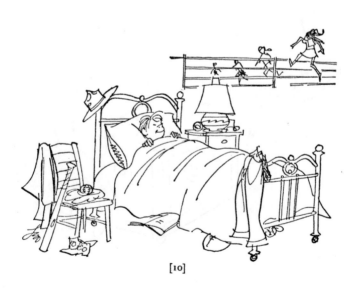

"No, I don't think so," I said, though I was still a little uncertain about a few things. I didn't want him to think me slow.

"Girls are all alike," he said. "They'll all do it. But you have to lead up to it just right."

"Sure," I said, not quite sure what I was so sure about. I narrowed my eyes a little, the way Carl did when he was being shrewd about something or the cigarette smoke was getting into his eyes.

"Well, good luck," Carl said, and he left the next day and I never saw him again.

I doubt that the girls in junior high school and, later, in high school, knew how much they were on my mind. I thought about them day and night. There was one, especially, whom I dreamt about for

four years, until I went away to college. She was a blonde, Cynthia Nugent, and she had the biggest breasts of any girl in school. Once I overheard my mother and father talking about her.

"Who is that blonde in junior high," my father asked, "the one who works Saturdays at the Emporium?"

"Do you mean Marylou Jesperson?" my mother said.

"No, I mean that other one. You know," my father hesitated a moment, "the one with the big breasts."

"Oh, so you've been looking," my mother said.

"The way they stick out," my father said defensively, "it's hard to see around them. Come on, who is she?"

"Why do you want to know?" my mother asked.

"I was just wondering," my father said. "It's hard to think of anyone that big in junior high."

"She's very mature for her age," my mother said.

"There wasn't anyone like that when *I* was in junior high," my father said, and he sounded wistful.

As I say, I dreamt about Cynthia almost every night. The dream I liked best was the one about Cynthia going with me to my mountain cabin and our being caught in a rainstorm and not having any dry clothes and having to put on dressing gowns and lie around on a bearskin rug in front of a roaring fire. Cynthia's dressing gown didn't fit very well, and she couldn't keep her breasts from popping out, there on the bearskin rug. No doubt my dream was influenced by a movie I had seen, when the hero and the heroine got caught in a rainstorm and didn't have any dry clothes to put on and all the rest. But it was very real to me, and I could hardly wait to go to bed and get to sleep and start dreaming.

Actually I never took Cynthia to my mountain cabin, partly because I had no mountain cabin and partly because I never even ate with her in the school cafeteria. We rarely exchanged a word. The longest and most personal conversation I ever had with her was the time I was sitting next to her in class and drawing the shape of her leg in my English notebook. I became so engrossed in this that I didn't notice she was leaning over and watching me, as I looked first at her leg and then at the sketch I was making.

"What are you doing?" she whispered.

I was so startled I dropped my pencil, which enabled me to smear the drawing a little with my sweaty hand as I leaned over to pick up my pencil.

"Nothing," I whispered back.

"You're drawing something. What's it supposed to be?"

I've never been a very quick thinker, but I was this time. While she was whispering, I kept on drawing, turning Cynthia's leg into the slightly leaning trunk of a palm tree, with branches where her knee had been. I made her foot into a little island. The whole thing was rather pretty, and I wish I had it today to frame and hang on my wall.

"See," I said, "a desert island."

"Oh," Cynthia said, and I have never known

whether she caught on or not. Anyhow, we had been making a little too much noise, and the English teacher, Miss Bingham, came over to me and pulled the page out of my notebook.

"A nice piece of work, Mr. Van Gogh," she said. "But you must be in the wrong class. This is English, not Art."

The class laughed, because Miss Bingham could be pretty funny, and it was a good idea to laugh even when she wasn't. Though the joke was on me, I didn't mind. The important thing was that Miss Bingham, who was waving my drawing in front of everybody, obviously thought it was a palm tree and not Cynthia's leg.

I realize now that I should have left it as Cynthia's leg and let Cynthia see it. She probably would have been pleased, since she had very nice legs, and there is no telling where we might have gone from there. But I missed out with Cynthia, just the way I missed out with Miss Webster and Lucille Briggs.

The trouble with me was that I was shy. This was not my only trouble. I was also the smallest boy in the class and I had more pimples than anybody except George Bruckhauser, who was really a mess. My mother and father said I would grow out of it in a few years and tried to keep me from eating chocolate, but George was so bad that his parents took him to the doctor for treatments that did no good whatsoever.

Nonetheless, even George Bruckhauser had a girl, and she wasn't bad looking, except for her teeth. Though I would have preferred Cynthia, I would have settled for George's girl, and I even dreamt about her a couple of times. Once I had one of those dreams about the mountain cabin and the rainstorm, and it was George's girl instead of Cynthia who was lying on the bearskin rug in front of the fire.

Finally, in my senior year at high school, I made a bold move toward conquest of Cynthia. I bought her a three-pound box of chocolates for Christmas. At last she would know how I felt about her and how much I was willing to spend on her. It might drive her into my arms.

The only trouble was, I didn't want to send the box of chocolates through the mail and have it all jounced around, and I didn't have the nerve to hand my present to her personally. So I paid a little kid in the neighborhood a quarter to deliver the box of chocolates to Cynthia's house.

No sooner had I dispatched the chocolate-bearer than I began to have misgivings. Perhaps I was being too forward, and Cynthia would be angry with me. Or, even worse, the chocolates might soften Cynthia up and she would really go for me, and then what would I do, since I was completely without experience? I wondered what had got into me, doing such a risky thing. That night I not only couldn't dream, I couldn't sleep.

Christmas came and went. I heard nothing from Cynthia. School started again after the vacation.

The first day of school, Ken Porteus, president of the student body, came up to me. Ken was a tall, handsome fellow who could eat chocolate bars without getting pimples. The girls were all crazy about him. If I could have been anybody in the world, it would have been Ken. He never paid much attention to me, and it was a thrill to see him coming right toward me now.

"Hi," he said, in his easy, confident way.

"Hi," I said, my voice coming out a little higher than I wished.

"Cynthia Nugent wanted me to ask you something," he said.

This was probably the greatest moment in my life, up to and including high school. Here was the president of the student body bringing me a personal message from the prettiest girl in school, the girl of my dreams. What could the message be? My heart pounded, my legs went weak, and I had a hard time getting my breath.

"O.K.," I said, trying to be nonchalant but having that curious feeling I had had once before, when I was in a mob scene in a play in my last year in junior high, holding a spear, and I fainted and they had to pull the curtain until they could revive me and/or drag me off the stage. I could imagine myself falling at Ken Porteus' feet in a dead faint. What would he think of me *then?* The only thing that kept me from fainting, I guess, was my curiosity about what Cynthia wanted Ken to ask me.

"Cynthia wonders about something," I could hear Ken saying, and his voice seemed to come from far away. "She received a three-pound box of chocolates for Christmas. There was a note inside that said this was a present from you, but she can't be-

[17]

lieve it. She says she hardly knows you and she doesn't see why you would be sending her a box of chocolates and somebody must be playing a joke on her or on you or something. What she wants to know is, you didn't really send her the chocolates, did you?"

"No," I said, "of course not." It had been a silly thing to do, and I was glad to get out of it so easily.

"That's what I said when she told me about it," Ken said. "She just wanted to check, to make sure. Anyhow, her boyfriend, Bob Cartright, gave her a box of chocolates too, so she gave this box to me. They're swell chocolates, and they must have cost somebody plenty. A pretty expensive joke, I'd say."

"Yes," I said, feeling more self-assured now, even as I was giving up Cynthia forever. "Some guys will do anything for a laugh."

That night I dreamt about the mountain cabin and the rainstorm again. Once again I was lying there in my dressing gown on the bearskin rug in front of the fire. But I was all alone.

Three

Everyone knows that the main reason for going to college is to get educated. That is, to learn whatever there is left to know about the opposite sex. Since I had learned so little up to this time, except second-hand from Carl Hawkins, I looked forward to college as the time when I would really get going. Besides, I now had a car, a one-seater where I could be alone with a girl without having another couple in the back seat spying on me, or distracting me. And my pimples were a lot better.

So I was all set. I was still shy and without technique, but I was getting desperate.

My first date was with a cute little redhead, Sue Billingsley. She was in Chemistry with me, and sometimes we performed experiments together in lab. I began to get ideas about performing experiments with her in my car, more biology than chemistry. Finally I got up the courage to ask her to go to a movie with me, and somewhat to my surprise she accepted. The movie was in another town, and this

provided an opportunity for a good drive, and parking somewhere on the way home.

This was the first date of my life. I had been slow,
but now I was going to make up for lost time. I
made the most careful preparations, including
spending most of the previous day scouting for a

good parking place. At last I found just the spot, on top of a hill where there was a turnoff from the road, a snug, romantic place under a large oak tree. I even carted off some papers and tin cans left by picnickers, so that there would be nothing to spoil the mood.

I picked up Sue at her dormitory. She looked cuter than ever, in a low-cut dress that just about matched her hair. When I got a whiff of her perfume as I helped her into the car, I trembled all over. This was it!

Not until I had driven several miles did I begin to realize what I was in for. Sue was a compulsive talker. She chattered a mile a minute. I hadn't noticed this in Chemistry lab, preoccupied as I was with washing out beakers or trying to pour acid without spilling it. And maybe it was only on a date that Sue yakked constantly. It must have been something psychological, perhaps a defense mechanism.

Sue talked all the way to the movie. Even during the movie she whispered until the people in front of us turned around and scowled and the people behind us said "Shush!" so loud that it bothered those who hadn't been bothered before. We left before the movie was over, Sue wanting to go where she could talk louder and I wanting to get into the car and head for that parking place.

We parked in the spot I had chosen, with the car

facing out where we could see the lights of the city below us. But I guess this was a mistake.

"Oh, look at all the lights. They're beautiful, aren't they?" Sue exclaimed.

"Yeah," I said, starting to grapple, a little clumsily.

"What do you suppose that building is over there, with all the lights around the top?"

"I dunno," I said, not even looking, my head being turned around. I was trying to plant a kiss, but Sue kept bobbing and craning to see the lights, and anyhow her lips were always moving.

"Oh!" she exclaimed once, when I had just about managed. She sounded so startled that I backed off, thinking maybe she had seen somebody come up to the car.

"What's the matter?"

"Look! See that long line of lights. They're moving. Do you suppose they could be cars?"

I never did manage to kiss Sue. I couldn't even hold her hand, she was so busy pointing out the lights. I could have kicked myself for choosing such a parking place. We drove back to the dormitory, Sue talking all the way about those lights.

"Good night," she said at the door, or it might have been "Good light," because I wasn't really listening. "I've had a wonderful evening."

I hadn't.

I took her out just once more, to make sure. This

time I parked where we faced right into the stony side of an embankment. No lights of the city, no view at all. But Sue never once stopped talking.

"Oh, look at all those layers of rocks!" she said. "My roommate's taking Geology, and she says. . . ."

This was my first, but not my last, experience with women who talk too much or at the wrong time. Years later, I read an item in the newspaper that said, "A woman's vocal cords vibrate twice as fast as a man's." By this time I was over my bitterness about Sue, jabbering away in that parked car about lights and Geology and whatnot, and so was fairly gentle in some lines I wrote:

> I'm grateful for having the truth at last,
>> It causes my harshness to soften.
> I wasn't aware it was twice as fast,
>> I thought it was twice as often.

My second date in college was very different. Not wishing to get talked out of it again, I was careful to pick a girl who hardly ever said anything. I checked on this carefully. Peg Borchert was as silent as they come. And not just in class. I talked with fellows who had been out with her, and they said she never said much but "Yes" and "No," and mostly "Yes." She was a looker, too, a tall, athletic brunette with a wonderful figure.

I had to ask Peg several times before I could

wangle a date with her. It was like getting an appointment with a dentist, she was so booked up. But finally she said all right, she would go with me on the class outing in the mountains. This was a good break for me because, while I wasn't very athletic, I was pretty competent at hiking, since it didn't take much skill to keep putting one foot in front of the other. I thought I might be able to impress Peg a bit with my stamina, and show her I was a more virile type than I looked. I might even rescue her if she got into trouble, and I planned to take along a first-aid kit to bandage her knee or whatever if she hurt herself. It was pretty rough going, up there in the mountains. Of course Peg herself was the outdoor type and keen on climbing over rocks and things. In fact my only objection to her was that she was taller than I, and had broader shoulders.

Once I mentioned her size to a fellow who had taken her out several times.

"She's pretty big," I said. "Isn't she kind of mannish?"

"Sure, there's a lot of her," he said, "but it's all in the right places. She's every inch a woman." He emphasized "every inch" and winked at me.

"She's going on the class outing up in the mountains with me," I said.

"Lucky guy," he said. "She's great stuff outdoors, even better than indoors. But you'd better wear some comfortable shoes. She'll walk the tail off you."

So I went on the outing with Peg. She was all bundled up in ski clothes, with a heavy sweater. It made her look bigger than ever, and yet good. Despite all the clothes, I could see she had quite a figure, and she was in her element, hiking around up in the mountains. I felt pretty proud of myself, having a date who fitted in so well and didn't have to be dragged along, like some of the girls.

We had walked several miles, Peg striding on ahead of everybody and I managing to stick pretty close behind her. Aside from not being able to catch up with her, what made me stay pretty close behind was her behind, which, in those ski pants, had me almost hypnotized. I couldn't take my eyes off that rear of hers and the rhythmical way it worked from side to side as she climbed up a mountain slope.

Maybe if I *had* taken my eyes off her, I wouldn't have come so close to losing my life.

We were climbing over some rocks near the top of a ridge, and I was watching what I had been watching instead of watching where I was going. I don't know what happened, but suddenly I went right over the side of a cliff. All I had the presence of mind to do was to scream.

Fortunately, I didn't go all the way to the pile of jagged rocks a couple of hundred feet below. In fact

I slid only five or six feet down before grabbing hold of the branch of a little tree that the Deity had put there for just such an emergency. As I clung there, praying, Peg looked over the edge at me.

"What are you doing down there?" she asked.

"Help me, I can't hang on much longer," I said, not thinking any explanation necessary.

"Why didn't you watch where you were going?"

"Help me, *please*," I said.

Though she was agonizingly slow about it, perhaps because she saw I was not in quite such a desperate situation as I thought, Peg finally took over.

"Put your foot on that crotch of the tree," she said, "and stand up straight. Then stretch out your hand to me. I think I can pull you up."

I did as she told me and she yanked me up over the side. It was almost embarrassingly easy.

"You were pretty scared, weren't you?" she said.

"Well, a little, maybe," I said, now safe on top.

"I've never seen anybody with such a ghastly look on his face," she said. "Well, let's go. They'll wonder where we are."

When I tried to stand up, I found I had twisted my ankle. I couldn't put my weight on it.

"I'm sorry," I said. "I'm afraid I can't walk."

Peg looked at me with more annoyance than sympathy. She was probably thinking, "Why did I have

[27]

to get mixed up with such a weakling? He's spoiling my hike."

I would have been satisfied if Peg had let me hold onto her while I hobbled down to where the cars were parked. But that would have been too slow for her, and she was not a woman for half measures.

"Well, here we go," she said, and she hoisted me over her shoulder, fireman's lift, and started down the mountain.

Can you imagine how I felt, carried like a sack of potatoes—by a girl?

When we got in sight of the members of the class, mostly sitting under trees necking, I asked Peg to set me down.

"I can walk the rest of the way," I said.

"No," she said, and she wasn't even breathing hard, "we wouldn't want that little foot to hurt, would we?"

I've never been so embarrassed in my life as I was when Peg lugged me, fireman's lift, right past all our classmates and dropped me into my car.

"Thank you very much," I said. "Let's go back to town. I guess you've had enough exercise for today."

"You go on," she said. "I can hike another hour or so before it gets dark. Maybe I can find some-body to go with me." She was looking straight at Clyde Harper, all-conference fullback, and he was looking back at her and smiling.

That was my second date in college, and my last.

Just two dates in four years, that's all I had. But from Peg I learned an important lesson about women. While you are looking at a woman's legs and all that sort of thing, take a peek at her shoulders. And feel her biceps. Never get mixed up with a woman who is stronger than you are. She might save your life, but it wouldn't be worth it.

When I graduated from college, I had never even kissed a girl. The closest I came was that time in the car with Sue Billingsley, when we were parked on top of the hill looking at the lights, and she talked her way out of it.

I had no more prospect of marriage than when I was eight, preoccupied with marbles.

Four

Until I was twenty-six years old my experience with women, in any meaningful way, was zero. I had read plenty, I had been told plenty, I had dreamed plenty, but I had done nothing. Such attempts as I had made, which I have already described, had ended in failure. I was an only child, and my parents were beginning to think I would be the last of the line. They longed for a daughter-in-law and grandchildren. I overheard them once and, when I discovered they were talking about me, I continued listening.

"It doesn't look as if he'll ever marry," my mother said.

"I wonder if there's something wrong with him," my father said.

"What do you mean?" my mother asked, her voice full of concern.

"You know what I mean," my father said.

"You don't really think so, do you?" my mother asked, now really worried.

"Well, by the time I was his age," my father said, "I had—"

"I'd just as soon not hear," my mother said. "You men are all alike, bragging about such things. Women have the good taste not to talk."

"Fifty percent of all the people who marry are women," my father said. "Of course there was the fellow who said that there really are three sexes: the male sex, the female sex, and insects."

"Quit your joking," my mother said. "We've got to find a wife for our son."

"What good would it do? You can lead a man to the altar but you can't make him take the vows. You aren't proposing we use force on the boy, are you?"

"If you'll get serious for a minute, perhaps we can work something out. At least we can make a try. Now I have this list. . . ."

That's as much as I heard, because my mother and father then went into a huddle over what I can only assume was a list of prospective daughters-in-law. All I know is that they picked out a girl who had been in school with me from first grade. To my parents, she had the most important of all qualifications: she was "nice." That means she came from a good family, was courteous to older people, went to church, didn't smoke, was never heard to use bad words, and never "got into trouble" with the boys. In grammar school I remembered her for her long

[31]

pigtails, the ends of which the boy who sat behind her was always dipping into his inkwell. In high school I had had her name on a list myself. It was a list of the girls who appealed to me most, the first of whom, of course, was Cynthia. Though I was too shy to do anything about it, I got a vicarious thrill out of carrying the list around. As I say, this girl my parents picked out for me was on it. She was last.

She was nice, all right. I guess the trouble was that she was too nice.

Once my mother and father had picked out this girl, they went to work. Their methods ranged from the subtle and wily to the obvious. The one emotion that marked their every effort was desperation. This, they were pretty sure, was the last chance.

By a strange coincidence, this girl's mother and father thought their daughter was just about over the hill, marriagewise. She was seven months older than I, and a woman who is twenty-six going on twenty-seven and hasn't yet snagged a man is pretty hopeless. She might as well resign herself to teaching school, which is what she had been doing for five years. And having been a schoolteacher for five years was another thing that just about ruled out any prospect of marriage.

My father was a man of action, and as soon as he and my mother had decided on this girl for me, he called up the girl's father and made him a proposition. Their conversation, I imagine, went something like this:

"We think it's about time our son got married," my father said, after the barest preliminaries.

"We think the same thing about our daughter," the girl's father said.

"Then how about their marrying each other?" my father suggested.

"A fine idea," the girl's father said. "Do what you can, and you can count on our help."

"Let's shake on it," my father said, forgetting he was talking over the telephone.

It was summer and I was home on vacation preparatory to taking a teaching post at a small Presbyterian college in the South. The two families had to work fast, and they did. They didn't let me in on it for fear I would louse things up, my record thus far having been so dismal. But the girl, whom they coached in daily skull sessions, was their most valuable accomplice.

"Be careful," her father said. "Don't show your hand."

"Show him a few other things, though," my father said, referring to a proposed trip to the beach. "But not too much. Keep him wanting to see more." My father knew what he was talking about. He once went to two strip tease shows the same day, with only a few minutes between for a sandwich and a cup of coffee to keep up his strength.

"Don't listen to him," my mother said. "The way to a man's heart is through his stomach. Invite him to dinner, just the two of you. Show him how well you can cook. I'll give you some recipes."

"Knit him a sweater," her mother said. "Or maybe, since time is short, make it a tie. There's nothing as feminine as knitting and sewing. Let him see you making your own dress, too, and he'll think you're a practical sort who'll save him a lot of money."

But as it turned out, the most effective thing wasn't contrived by our parents. It was the providential place of our meeting, by sheer accident, for the first time in several years—in fact since we were in college together. Both of us had been away studying and working, and even when we had been home on visits our paths hadn't crossed. We met in a bakery, where I had gone for some doughnuts and where the girl was at that moment buying some sweet rolls. My first glimpse of her, after all those years, was over a tray of cream puffs.

I always become sentimental, if not downright passionate, in a bakery, and have stood for several minutes swaying slightly in a kind of delirium in front of a row of freshly baked chocolate eclairs. So when I looked at that girl over the cream puffs, with the aroma of doughnuts rising from the bag in my hand to my quivering nostrils, a great hunger came over me. It was love at first whiff.

From then on, it was all downhill. The home

cooking, the knitting and sewing, the artful display of a knee one day, a bit of cleavage the next—these all had their effect. But they were unnecessary. I wanted to marry the girl as soon as I saw her in the bakery. But I couldn't get up the courage to ask her. I couldn't believe she would marry *me*, the oaf who had failed so completely with women since he was eight years old.

How was I to know that she not only was fearful of becoming an old maid, but for some strange reason really liked me? How was I to know that the two families were in league to make the match? I should have got the idea after about the sixth dinner she cooked for me with all my favorite dishes. I should have suspected something when my father said things like, "She'll make some man a fine wife!" and "I've always thought it would be nice if our two families could get together some way." But I just thought the girl liked to cook and sew, and I knew my father liked to talk. I wasn't going to ask and get turned down.

So, at the end of the summer, I left home without popping the question. Nothing ventured, nothing lost, and all that sort of thing. I have never been much at taking risks. But the summer had not been a total loss. I had gained twelve pounds from all that good cooking. And, skinny as I was, I could use it. It made me feel more of a man, going from a fourteen and a half to a size fifteen collar.

At this little college in the South, where I was Professor of English and Chairman of the Department at twenty-six (which should indicate that this institution was not Tulane University or the University of Georgia), I had some additional duties to make me worth my salary of $2,000. The most additional duty was being proctor of the men's dormitory. In this capacity I was, without having the official title, virtual Dean of Men, since all of the male students lived there, the college had no Dean of Men, and I was in charge.

The proctor lived in the dormitory too, in what was laughingly referred to as a suite: a small study, a small bedroom, a small bathroom, and a small closet. Fortunately, I was pretty small myself, even with a size fifteen collar.

One of the favorite games on this campus was an ingenious sport known as Getting Rid of the Proctor. The students usually made the first move, something cautious like putting a cow in the proctor's room while he was at dinner. The proctor might retaliate by complaining to the Prexy. Then the students would escalate by swishing a bucket of water under the proctor's door so that it would make his rug soggy. Having run out of clever moves, he would get back at them with another complaint to the Prexy. This encouraged the students, sensing victory, to put on the pressure. Playing the game with the proctor before me, they had lit giant fire-

crackers in the middle of the night and skillfully rolled them down the corridor so they would explode in front of his bedroom door. And they had shaved his white cat and painted it with Mercurochrome and left it to run yowling across the campus, scared crazy.

The last move, though, was always up to the proctor. At the end of the year he moved out. Up to my time, no proctor had lasted longer than a year.

My predecessor had been the football coach. If they could get rid of him, the students thought, after looking me over and at least in their imagination feeling my biceps and trying to find my pulse, I would be easy. They were right.

One month after I became proctor, I made an important decision. I was not going to serve only a year, like the proctors before me. I was going to serve only a month. For the sake of my health and sanity, I was getting out of that dormitory and moving to an apartment immediately. As I started to pack up, I came across my contract, which I had read only perfunctorily before accepting the position. (This was during the Depression, and I was glad to have a job at any salary, under any conditions.) Reading the fine print, I discovered that as long as I was unmarried I must serve as proctor and *live in the men's dormitory*. Of course if I were married, I couldn't live there if I wanted to.

The solution was obvious, even to me. I got off a

wire to the girl at home: WILL YOU MARRY ME AT CHRISTMAS? CAN'T LIVE ANY LONGER WITHOUT YOU. I didn't explain that I couldn't live with her, either, in the men's dormitory. It may have been a little terse, but it sounded as though I really needed her, and I did.

Her reply came back the next day. Apparently it did not take her long to decide. She also was caught in a bad situation, teaching a roomful of brats in grammar school, and I had offered her a good way out. YES, her wire read. I CAN HARDLY WAIT.

I made it until the Christmas vacation, barricading my doors and wearing earplugs. Not wishing to raise any questions about the terms of my contract, I decided not to tell the Prexy until after the wedding. But I had the wire all written out and ready to send: SORRY CAN'T LIVE IN MEN'S DORMITORY SECOND SEMESTER. NOT A PROPER PLACE FOR MY WIFE. HAPPY NEW YEAR.

I have always been grateful to the students of that college and their wide streak of sadism. Otherwise I might never have married.

Five

We were married on Christmas Day, for several very good reasons. First, it was in the Christmas vacation, with a week remaining for a honeymoon before getting back to the college and the wrath of the Prexy, tempered, I hoped, by my proposal of a system of student government that would make a proctor unnecessary. Second, it should help me, in the years ahead, remember the date of my wedding anniversary. Third, as I figured it, one present to my wife would serve two purposes. I have never regretted this choice of a date, and I commend it to others.

We had a civil ceremony. That is, everyone was civil to everyone else, in fact on extra good behavior. Actually we had a preacher perform the ceremony, and the wedding was held in the home of my wife-to-be. Why it was held in her home instead of at a church, I am not sure. Perhaps our two families had so few friends that they wouldn't make a respectable showing in the church. It's always embarrassing at either a wedding or a funeral not to have a good crowd. My father was especially sensitive about this sort of thing, and I could imagine him worriedly counting the house.

Another reason for our home wedding was that at the church it would have been open to everyone. At home, we could limit the attendance, explaining that there was room for only the immediate families. This way we could keep out the riffraff on my mother's side of the family, who would only have made trouble.

"It'll be a relief not to have your cousin Gracie and her loudmouth husband," was the way my father put it to my mother.

"If they're not invited, we won't have to include your oddball Uncle Herbert," my mother said.

We still had to have a few who were such close relatives that they couldn't be excluded. What we needed was some other criteria, such as an IQ test. But our guests conducted themselves better than anyone expected, perhaps awed by the seriousness of the situation. They probably would have behaved in the same restrained way in an operating room watching major surgery.

But the main reason for having a home wedding was, I am reasonably sure, to save money.

"Why pay twenty-five dollars for use of the church," a relative of my mother's said, "when it would only go to some missionary in Africa, trying to get the poor savages to wear hot, uncomfortable clothes."

As a matter of fact, I would have preferred a church wedding. It would have seemed more authentic, more like the real thing. Both families were churchgoers, too, except my father, who worked so hard all week he thought he was entitled to sleep on Sunday, and he believed it better to sleep on the couch in the den than in a hard wooden pew.

Anyhow, we had a home wedding, and it went off very well, except that the cloying odor of flowers was overpowering in that small living room. My mind wandered once during the service, and I forgot where I was and started looking around for the pallbearers.

I said "I do," and she said "I do," and the minister said "I now pronounce you man and wife," and it was all over. I kissed my bride, and was pleased to discover it was just as good as before we were married. It was reassuring to think that whatever my wife and I did together, from now on, would be legal.

The most memorable part of the marriage ceremony, to me, was something that happened shortly after the minister pronounced us man and wife and I kissed my bride. Wishing to pay up, as soon as I could get the minister alone I took an envelope out of my pocket and handed it to him.

"Thank you for marrying us," I said. "Here's a little something for you." I called it a little something, but I really thought it was pretty good pay

for about five minutes' work. Let me remind you that this was in 1932, during the Depression, when every dollar helped.

"Not at all. It was my pleasure," the minister said, taking the envelope as if he really hadn't expected a thing but would accept it if I insisted. He then stuffed the envelope casually into his outside coat pocket and seemed to forget about it. Excusing himself, he went into another room, away from the crowd. I assumed he sought a moment of solitude, perhaps to offer a prayer for the young couple. As my eyes followed him, I felt an upsurge of admiration for this man of the cloth and was ashamed of my own petty materialism.

What I then saw was disillusioning. The minister had his back turned to me, but because of a positioning of mirrors of which he was unaware, I could see what he did. Only seconds after leaving me he fished the envelope out of his pocket, nervously tore it open, and extracted the bill inside. Immediately his shoulders sagged, his head bent forward. The envelope dropped from his nerveless hands. Poor fellow. Obviously he had expected at least twice as much.

But he knew how to cope with disappointment. In a matter of minutes he had composed himself and joined the happy company. Coming up to me, he was completely at ease and able to flash a broad smile.

[44]

"A beautiful, beautiful wedding," he said, shaking my hand vigorously. "I wish you much happiness."

At first I had been annoyed at his haste in opening the envelope. Now I couldn't help admiring his resilience.

In fact I amazed myself. I wished I had given him more.

After the reception, we drove off for a short honeymoon at a nearby resort hotel. If you think I'm going to tell you all the details of our honeymoon, you have another think coming. Two things, however, I shall never forget. One is that when my wife and I opened the door of the elevator and stepped out into the lobby of the hotel the morning after our first night together, I found myself face to face with a friend of my father's. He recognized me at once and called me by name.

"Well, hello," he said. "What are you doing here?" The moment he said this, he noticed the attractive young lady with me.

"Meet Miss Stevens," I said without thinking, which is the way I say a good many things.

I suppose I should have explained that this was her maiden name, but he gave me no chance. Mumbling something, he left like a shot. Apparently I had answered his question.

The other memorable thing about my honeymoon was that I had a terrible cold.

Six

That was thirty-five years ago. I have had a good many colds since then, but only one wife.

Even with more than a third of a century of experience, I do not claim to be an authority on marriage. I do not even claim to be an authority on my wife. I am still studying, still learning. Some of the results of my study will be related in the pages that follow.

One reason I got married, I suppose, was to get some good home cooking. I was tired of eating at restaurants and paying restaurant prices. However I must admit that, after my marriage, I missed the waitresses.

My wife, who can see right through me, knows what I am thinking about when I sit there with a far-away look, toying with my food. Wishing me to be happy, she is always in there trying. One day just before dinner she handed me a neatly typed menu.

"What would you like?" she asked. She was dressed in a uniform of sorts, a Swiss costume she had brought back from Europe, and she had an order pad and a pencil in her hand and was chewing gum. "The chicken livers are very nice."

"How is the veal cutlet?" I asked, entering into the spirit of the thing.

"Very nice," she said.

"And the roast lamb?"

"Very nice."

"And how are the lamb chops?"

"Very nice."

"I think I'll take the tenderloin tips."

"We're out of tenderloin tips. They should of been crossed off."

It was just like old times, especially when, after bringing me my food, my wife disappeared into the

kitchen, or went next door, and I couldn't get her back to fill my water glass, even though I yelled and beat on the table.

Through the years, we have played this little restaurant game about twice a month. It makes me more content to have given up my old life. We balk at only a couple of things. I won't pay the bill my wife brings on a tray, and she won't go topless. Each of us yields a little, however, in the interest of harmony. I leave her a small tip and she wears a low-cut dress.

My wife is an excellent cook. Not as good as her mother, as I try to keep from telling her, but plenty good. Perhaps if I were a gourmet type, I would appreciate her more, but I am a steak-and-potatoes man. I could eat my favorite dishes every day, or at least twice a week. But she considers her kitchen a laboratory, and likes to experiment.

"What's this?" I asked her one day when she put an odd-looking dish before me. It was some sort of casserole, slightly greenish, with melted cheese on top. I wasn't sure whether to eat it with a fork or a spoon or, indeed, whether to eat it at all.

"Go ahead and try it," she said. "It's a new recipe. If you like it, I'll serve it to the Wednesday Club next week."

In the old days a king had a royal taster, to make sure he could eat and drink without being poisoned by a rival for the throne. Now wives have husbands for much the same purpose. With this casserole, as has become my practice, I ate just enough to give a verdict—not one morsel more. The trick is to eat enough that you might get sick but won't die.

The casserole wasn't too bad. It had no distinctive taste, which at least is better than having an unpleasant taste. I got it down and kept it down, and that made it acceptable for the Wednesday Club. Women, after all, are less concerned about whether a dish is good than whether it is different.

My wife is constantly in search of new recipes, the way scientists are constantly in search of a cure for the common cold. Though she often wheedles a recipe out of people with whom we dine, this is only to make her hostess feel good, and she has no intention of using it. Her most valued recipes come from exotic cookbooks, such as the one privately printed by a one-hundred-year-old Tennessee woman, and the one translated from the Turkish, said to contain the favorite recipes of a famous Sultan and to be responsible for his astonishing sexual prowess, even at my age.

As for my wife's love of cookbooks, let me put it in verse:

> My wife reads cookbooks as if they
> Were novels. She can sit all day,

A cookbook in her hand, engrossed,
Unmoving, silent as a post,
Except for cheeks now flushed, now white,
And little shudders of delight.
Ingredients are characters,
And recipes are plots, good sirs,
And words like "heaping tablespoon"
Can very nearly make her swoon.
Oh, Hollywood may yet find means
To film a cookbook, full of scenes
Of high adventure, passions, crimes.
My wife will go a dozen times.

When I eat best is when we have guests for dinner. After a week or so of ground round, stew, and questionable experiments, it's a thrill to have filet mignon. My taste buds, which have been dying on the vine, suddenly blossom again. But I must pay for my pleasure: not only the enormous grocery bill but the slave labor involved in lugging extra chairs from the bedroom, putting in table leaves, dusting places my wife can't reach (and no one but a giraffe or a basketball player could see), and tidying up the yard. When we are preparing for a dinner party, my wife assumes the pose of a straw boss or a foreman at the docks.

"Put it over here," she says.

"No," she says, after a moment's thought, "put it over there."

"Lift that rug."

"Turn that table."

"Push that chair."

"Pull that curtain."

Some day I expect her to say, in the same tone, "Tote that barge, lift that bale."

Late into the night, after our guests have gone, I reverse the actions described above, restoring everything to the familiar pattern of everyday living.

We have two groups of friends: those we "owe" and those we "don't owe." This has nothing to do with money. It is a matter of who had whom last. My wife has a list, which she keeps more carefully than her checkbook.

"We owe the Hadleys, the Millers, the Redpaths, and the Osgoods," she said on a typical evening, looking up from her worksheet.

"Then let's have them all over next Saturday night," I said. "With us, that will make ten. Just a nice size for a dinner party."

"But the Hadleys wouldn't go with the Redpaths and the Millers wouldn't go with the Osgoods," my wife said. I had forgotten this other list of my wife's, the list of who will "go" with whom. I know only the general principles, such as not mixing Republicans with Democrats and ex-wives with ex-husbands. My wife is aware of the finer points.

"Didn't you know that Mary Osgood and Dot Miller had a run-in at the supermarket when Mary took the last can of artichoke hearts, and they haven't been speaking since?"

"I suppose you mean they haven't been speaking *to* each other," I said, never passing up a chance to correct my wife's English, there being little enough I can do for her. "I can't imagine either of them keeping still for long."

Considering how many of our friends won't go with other of our friends, it's a wonder we can ever get together a dinner party. It's also a wonder we could like so many people who don't like each other.

I would love to have a peek at our friends' lists, to see what people they think *we* wouldn't go with. But perhaps it is just as well I shall never see these lists, since they might be embarrassingly long.

Usually my wife is content to eat at home. This way, she doesn't miss her favorite TV program. But now and then she suggests we eat at some new restaurant she has heard of, a place with low lights and high prices. Occasionally I take the initiative myself, to show I'm not stingy.

"How about eating out tonight?" I ask, when I've come home from work and am sure she has dinner cooking. This is one way you can have your cake and eat it too, though you may not enjoy it—not if your wife can make you feel as cheap as my wife can make me.

But sometimes, despite everything, we eat at a fancy restaurant, just the two of us. After a beautifully served dinner, we both feel pretty mellow and affectionate. Seen by candlelight and through a centerpiece of flowers, we look better than usual to each other.

"You know," my wife says, "you look distinguished." This is the most she ever says—not that I look handsome but that I look distinguished, which could simply mean that I have the kind of face people remember even if they try to forget. But I take it as a compliment and reach through the greenery and clasp my wife's hand, at the risk of having hot wax drip onto my arm.

These are the moments when I should say something romantic, maybe quote from John Donne or Omar Khayyám. But I always come up with the wrong thing and break the spell.

"Darling," I say, "why can't you learn to cook like that?"

There are times, I have learned, when a husband should hold his wife's hand, look at her adoringly, and keep his mouth shut.

Seven

We have never had an aged or indigent member of my family or my wife's family living with us. When this possibility first came up, I put my foot down. Sometimes when I put my foot down my wife's foot is under it.

"No," I said tersely.

"Why not?" my wife asked. "It would be cheaper than paying the bills at a rest home."

"Some things are more important than money," I said.

"Well, that's a switch," my wife said. "I never thought I would hear you say a thing like that. Would you repeat what you just said?"

"Some things are more important than money." This time I thought before I spoke, and I had to strain a little to get the words out. However, I recognized it as a noble sentiment and was a little proud of myself.

"Name one thing," my wife said, "that is more important than money—to you."

"Peace of mind," I said. "And you can't have peace of mind in your home if it's full of free loaders complaining about the accommodations and spying on you."

"I'm going to tell you something that will surprise you," my wife said.

"What's that?"

"I agree with you."

We have our little disagreements, but here was a big agreement. Probably nothing has contributed so much to the success of our marriage. I say this after having listened to some of our friends. Take Phil Bascomb.

"My wife's Aunt Sarah has been living with us three years now," he told me one day, "and I've just about had it."

"What's the trouble, Phil?" I asked. "She has always seemed a nice, congenial lady to me."

"That's a laugh," he said. "She's all right for a few minutes, maybe an hour. But *three years!*"

"What does she do that bothers you so much?"

"It isn't what she does, it's what she doesn't do. She doesn't get up when we do. She doesn't help around the house. She doesn't turn off the lights when she goes to bed. She doesn't move from in front of the TV. In fact the worst part of it all is that she doesn't move, period."

"What does your wife think of her? She's *her* aunt, isn't she?"

"My wife doesn't think, she feels. She feels sorry for the woman because we are her only relatives. I feel sorry for us because we have a relative like Aunt Sarah. I know how the Ancient Mariner felt, with an albatross around his neck. Only his dropped off after a while, and I think I've got Aunt Sarah for life. The only hopeful thing is that I may not live too long, thanks to that woman."

I detected a note of bitterness in Phil's voice. Actually, he doesn't know how lucky he is, having to put up with one of his wife's relatives. It might have been a relative on *his* side of the family. That is far worse, because you can't blame someone else.

Though, as I say, we have had no in-laws living with us, we have had them for short visits, such as overnight. Anything more than overnight I consider a long visit. There is, for instance, an elderly person who visits us about twice a year. Ashamed though I am, I must confess that she is a relative of mine, not my wife's, as my wife never fails to mention.

This woman usually arrives about noon on Saturday, in time for lunch, and leaves on Sunday, after dinner. We would manage to be away, except that we can't tell when she is coming and we can't go out of town *every* weekend in order not to be home when she comes. Usually I get a phone call.

"I'm here," a voice says.

"Who's where?" I ask, hoping it's not who I think it is, or that it's who I think it is but she is at her home, two hundred miles away, and about to explain why she is not coming to visit us.

"I'm at the bus depot," she says, after she has confirmed my fears that she is who she is. "You can pick me up any time."

The bus depot is six miles away, through traffic, and I drive slowly, for safety's sake and to put off meeting the woman as long as possible. As I drive along, I think about this creature who will soon be under our roof, in the bosom of our family. She has had two husbands. One of them died and the other is presumed dead. This second husband simply disappeared one day and has never been heard from since. How this woman ever got two husbands is beyond me. I think she put something in their drinks and propped them up during the wedding ceremony. She is tall and very thin, and I think starves herself between visits to us so that she will be able, as my wife says, "to eat us out of house and home." I have no idea how she supports herself. Yes, I do have an idea, though I wish I didn't. Several years ago she had a number of gold teeth that I looked at with fascination every time she opened her mouth, which was all too frequently. Lately I have noticed that on each visit she has one gold tooth fewer. Obviously she is cashing them in, one at a time. Some pawn shop must have a nice collection of molars and bicuspids.

Anyhow, I pick her up at the bus depot and take her home. She has only one small suitcase, which calms my mounting fear that she may have come to live with us.

"I'll drive you back to the bus depot tomorrow afternoon," I say hopefully. "Early Monday morning we're leaving on a little trip and we're closing up the house." I have never been very good at lying, but with practice I am improving.

One of the most amazing things about this woman is how much stuff she can pack into one suitcase, and how far she can make it go in messing up our house. Within twenty minutes she has scattered clothing and personal effects not only all over her bedroom but as far afield as the dining room and kitchen. Yet her suitcase still looks full. There's something creepy about it.

"Make yourself at home," I tell her, and this is a mistake. I have never been in her home, but I can guess what it is like.

"Is this yours?" I ask her, handing her one stocking gone astray from its mate. I know very well it's hers, but want to make her squirm a little.

"Why, yes it is," she says. "Where did you find it?"

"On the kitchen sink. We're having a casserole tonight, and I guess the other one is already inside."

"You're joking," she says, taking her stocking. But that night at dinner I notice her picking around on her plate at what look like nylon fibers.

Sunday afternoon finally arrives, and I drive our houseguest to the bus depot. Once I have seen her onto the bus and waved an enthusiastic good-bye, I head back for home, vastly relieved. I turn on the car radio and listen to the news: two plane crashes, a shipwreck, a fire, a strike, a couple of riots, and

threats of a major war. After all, it's Sunday, and things are pretty quiet.

"Can you find a cardboard box?" my wife asks as I come in from the garage.

"What do you want a box for?"

"She forgot a pair of shoes and a slip."

"And I suppose we have to wrap up the box and take it to the post office and pay the postage?"

"Yes, but it won't be as heavy as the travel iron and the jar of cold cream she left last time."

A man's home is his castle, and sometimes I wish mine had a moat and a drawbridge.

Eight

My wife likes to tell people, "We waited nine years for our first child." This embarrasses me, because it sounds as if we just sat around and waited, still believing in the stork and all that sort of thing. As a matter of fact we did everything we could, and had quite a bit of coaching from friends who had had children with no trouble at all, even when they didn't want them.

When it looked as if we were going to be childless, my wife got the idea of adopting a baby. I resisted any such crazy notion.

"If I can't have a child of my own, I don't want one," I said stubbornly. "Anyhow, you can't tell what we might get."

"You can't tell what we might get if we had a child of our own," my wife said. "There's an agency that finds children with the same physical characteristics and the same family background as the prospective parents. They could probably get us a baby whose father was an English professor and had droopy eyelids and a nose shaped like yours."

"No," I said. "Absolutely not. People would get the idea I had been philandering and we had adopted an illegitimate child of mine. As for my eyes and nose, why go out of your way to perpetuate my worst features?"

We argued about this for most of a year until my wife finally wore me down.

"All right," I said, "if it will make you happy." Actually I was beginning to incline toward the idea myself, but didn't want to admit it. I hate to lose face, having so little of it left.

So we filled out all sorts of forms and made an

appointment with the adoption agency for an interview.

I still remember the two hours we spent at the agency being interviewed by the woman who dispensed babies.

"Why can't you have a child of your own?" she asked.

"That's a pretty personal question, isn't it?" I said.

"I am certificated," she said. "You can tell me anything."

"Actually it's my wife's fault," I said.

"Have you had her tubes blown out?"

"Yes," I said, ready to blow a gasket myself.

"Well," she said, "I was hoping you could have your own child, because the supply of children up for adoption is far behind the demand."

"How long will we have to wait?" I asked.

"Assuming you meet all the qualifications, and I must still reserve judgment on that, it would be at least a year."

"A year!" I exclaimed. "Why, I thought we could pick up a baby today, while we are here. We already have the crib and blankets and everything."

"We really didn't think it would be more than a few weeks," my wife added.

"You will be lucky if a child is available in a year. It might be nearer a year and a half. There is a long waiting list."

My wife and I left the adoption agency pretty discouraged. I wasn't lukewarm any longer. I was eager to adopt a child, now that I found it was so difficult.

"Do you think we should try some other agencies?" I asked.

"I'm afraid it would be the same story everywhere, and I hate to fill out any more blanks," my wife said. "We've waited more than eight years now. We can wait another year."

But, as it turned out, we didn't have to wait a year. We went on a vacation right after that, and it must have been something in the water at this resort where we were staying. In a month my wife discovered she was pregnant.

We informed the adoption agency at once. Enclosing a check for all the trouble they had gone to, I wrote: "Thank you for trying to help us. You had said you might have a baby for us in a year. We think we can get one in nine months."

There was a good deal of talk in our little college town when it was discovered we were going to have a baby.

I had to take some ribald ribbing from friends of mine. College professors, I have discovered, have dirty minds.

"I thought you were too busy correcting papers," said one of them, a professor of Sociology who, even then, was worried about the population explosion.

He himself had four children.

Another colleague, a little sour ever since he failed to get tenure, approached it from another angle.

"It's pretty early yet to be sure," he said. "There's always the chance of a miscarriage."

This fellow was in Art History, specializing in the Middle Ages, and a bachelor at that. So his warning didn't carry much weight. I was fairly sure the baby would be born, but thought it might have three arms or no ears or some other deformity. I had heard that a child might be born misshapen because of the sins of its parents, and while I had not actually done anything bad, I had had some pretty evil thoughts, especially when I was in high school.

It was with considerable relief, then, that when the baby arrived I heard the doctor pronounce it normal. When I got my first look, I immediately counted the arms and checked both sides of the head to be sure there were ears. The infant seemed to have all the parts, and in the right number. If I was to be punished for my evil thoughts, it would be some other way.

It was a boy. This gave an extra boost to my feeling of virility, especially after I learned that the father determines the sex of the child. Never having had much hair on my chest, I was glad to have this sort of assurance.

Knowing how important it was to get the right

name for the boy, since it would be with him for life, my wife and I went into the matter thoroughly. We even bought a book, *Naming Your Baby*, which had hundreds of suggestions, so many that we became utterly confused.

"Let's name him after my father," my wife finally said.

"Then my father would feel hurt," I said.

"Let's name him after you," she said, and I thought it was sweet of her and for a moment weakened.

"No," I said after thinking it over. "We would always be getting our mail mixed up."

It was now five days after the boy was born, and it made us uncomfortable calling him "It" and putting off our friends who kept asking, "Haven't you named that baby of yours yet?" We are both indecisive, and it seemed possible that the lad would grow up nameless, signing himself "X." We thought of having a Name-the-Baby contest, requiring entrants to submit twenty-five cents and a box top.

Then I took the plunge. I decided to call him Geoffrey, after Geoffrey Chaucer, my favorite poet and the subject of a course I had taught for many years.

"Oh, all right," my wife said, none too enthusiastic but glad to have it decided.

Unfortunately, our son has never liked his name. People pronounce it "Guffry" and "Gee-o-free." Or they think he is putting on airs and pretending to be British. He wishes he had been named something ordinary and masculine and American, like John.

"You and your old Chaucer," he said to me once, looking at me reproachfully. "At least you might have named me William, after Shakespeare, and I could have been called Bill." For a while he threatened to go to court and change his name legally, but he decided an easier way was simply to use his initials. Now he signs himself G. S. Armour or G. Stevens Armour.

My wife and I admit we made a mistake. That is, I made it and she let me.

Having at last had one child, we found it no trouble at all to have another. Apparently we had got the combination. I don't know what we did differently, but there must be a little trick to it. It's like riding a bicycle. Once you learn how, you never forget. I guess we could have gone on and on, but we started rather late and decided to quit after the next one, especially since it was a girl and we now had one of each.

This time we had no difficulty deciding upon a name. In fact we had had the name for several years and could hardly wait to have a girl in order to give it to her. We might not even have had a second child but for the fact that we had this name lying around and it seemed a shame to waste it.

The name Karin might seem unexciting enough.

But it was the way we put it together that was to provide us with a conversation piece for years to come. You see, the "Ka" is for my wife's name, Kathleen, the "ri" is for my name, Richard, and the "n" is for nothing. Many people think this ingenious, or so they tell us, knowing we will agree with them. When I explain how we put the word "Karin" together, I always pause a little before say-

ing, "And the 'n' is for nothing." From much practice, I have the timing just right.

People usually misspell Karin. They are sure it is Karen and they think we are the ones who misspell it. She wishes her name were Jane.

Children are supposed to help hold a marriage together. They do this in a number of ways. For instance, they demand so much attention that a husband and wife, concentrating on their children, fail to notice each other's faults. Or, especially while the children are adolescents, parents are driven protectively into each other's arms—like two settlers of the Old West, huddled together while the redskins circle around them. Their consoling words, oft repeated, are: "Well, we still have each other."

"Children are the cement in a marriage," says my wife, who is a great one for aphorisms, proverbs, and metaphorical expressions.

All I know is that my wife is a brick, and we are stuck.

Nine

Women, I think, are more generous than men, especially when what they are giving away isn't money. My wife, for instance, is a little careful about how many dollars she donates to a charity in which we are only mildly interested, but she will unquestioningly drive our gas-guzzling car on numerous stop-and-start errands, and stand for hours in a gaily decorated booth, getting runs in her stockings and stretching her girdle out of shape. Even if her time is worth only a dollar an hour, which is well below the minimum wage prescribed by law, she will give twenty-four dollars worth of her time in three eight-hour days and think nothing of it.

Giving goods and services is relatively painless for my wife, just as it is easier for her to pay by check than by cash and easiest of all to charge something. I admit that I have a similar weakness as regards money substitutes, but I am not quite in the same class as my wife, I hope. Of one thing I am certain. She is more susceptible than I am to a fiendish tactic

employed by people who sell the things she buys. I can put it more succinctly in verse:

My wife, a woman whom I adore,
Thinks three-ninety-five is far less than four.
What is priced at four she would think
  outrageous
If she saw the ad in the paper's pageous,
But at three-ninety-five she would likely feel
The item a bargain, an outright steal.
This five-cent saving delights my wife—
And has kept me poor all our married life.

But let me go back to the matter of charity. From time to time we go through our closets to find items for the Disabled War Veterans or the Salvation Army or some other worthy organization. It's a nice way to be philanthropic without putting out any

cash, and at the same time to make a little room in our crowded closets.

It is, moreover, a time of discovery.

Recently, while looking for shirts I had outgrown (my arms have stayed the same length but my neck has expanded from a size fifteen to a fifteen and a half), I found a letter I had been trying to find for a long time. It wasn't the letter I wanted, it was the stamp on the envelope. It was an uncanceled stamp, as good as new, and I hate to waste anything. How long it had been since I misplaced that letter with the perfectly good stamp is indicated by the fact that I found it in the pocket of a shirt with a size fifteen collar.

Anyhow, I found it, and within five minutes of steaming and scraping had the stamp off—a little thin and curled, but usable. Lest you think me cheap, I should add that it was not an ordinary stamp, it was an airmail.

Another time, in the pocket of a sport jacket I was giving away because it was perfectly good except for a hole in one elbow, I found a dime. This was a thrill, because although I find all sorts of things, I seldom find money. It also shows how important it is to go through the pockets carefully before giving anything away. I don't know how the dime got there, because I never carry money around loose, being afraid of pickpockets and the like. As I placed the dime in my coin purse and buttoned the flap securely, I cautioned myself never to be so careless again.

Going through our closets to find things for charity is, as I have said, a time of discovery. Not only do I find articles I had given up for lost and perhaps already collected insurance on, but I find out things about my wife. I find, for instance, what an odd mixture of generosity and stinginess she is.

Once she insisted that I give away a pair of slacks that I had worn to paint the fence. Even the cleaner had given up on the paint spots. The last time we got the slacks back from the cleaner, after begging him to have another try, they were returned with a note saying, "Impossible."

"You'll never wear these again," my wife said, putting them into the Salvation Army box.

"You can't tell," I said, taking them out. "Slacks

with paint spots may be all the style one of these days."

"Don't be silly," my wife said, putting them back into the box. "You'll never wear them, and they just take up room."

"But if I won't wear them, who will?" I asked. "It's insulting to give anyone these slacks. Nobody's that hard up."

Eventually I won out and kept the slacks. The way I did it was to leave them in the box when I carried it out in front of the garage. Then, when my wife wasn't looking, I lifted the slacks out of the box and carried them back to my closet. True, I haven't worn them yet, but it gives me a comfortable feeling to know they are available, hanging under some good slacks so my wife is none the wiser.

On the other hand, my wife can be frightfully stingy, especially about some of her own things. Take shoes. She has eighteen pairs. I counted them. They fill a couple of shoe racks and spill over onto the floor. Not to mention the shoes under the bed and the ones in the back of the car.

"Why don't you get rid of a few pairs of shoes?" I asked her, holding out the Salvation Army box temptingly.

"I'd like to," she said, "but I haven't any I can spare."

"Do you mean to tell me you have to have eighteen pairs of shoes?" I said.

"I don't have eighteen pairs of shoes," she said, a little huffily.

"Yes, you do," I said. "In fact there are nineteen pairs, counting the ones you have on." Generously, I didn't mention the ones under the bed and in the back of the car.

Apparently she had never counted her pairs of

shoes, which seems strange to me. I know how many pairs I have.

"I have to have shoes to match my dresses," she said. "White and gold and blue and all the rest. You can get along with just black shoes and brown shoes. Give away some of your own shoes, if you want, but let mine alone."

"But think of the people who don't have even one decent pair of shoes," I said, shaming her. "You ought to share, even if it means a little sacrifice."

"People who haven't one pair of shoes probably like going barefoot," she said. "I'd like to go barefoot myself, but you'd be the first to complain. Besides, anybody who isn't used to wearing shoes would have a hard time getting into a size $7\frac{1}{2}$AA."

There's just one thing my wife and I are agreed on. We like to clean out our son's and daughter's closets.

"Here's a skirt Karin will never wear again," my wife says.

"And here's a jacket Jeff doesn't need any more," I say, after trying it on to make sure it is, as I feared, entirely too large for me.

Though her contributions are small, a fact which I applaud, my wife has entirely too many pet charities.

"We can give a little to each," she says. "Not much, but just a little."

"We can't give to everybody," I tell her. "Just

think, if we gave only one cent to each person in the United States we would be out about two million dollars, which isn't chicken feed."

"You know I don't mean *everybody*," she says. "I mean the people who are so needy that they swallow their pride and ask us."

There's no use arguing with her. I swallow a little hard myself, and write another check.

My wife has the curious belief, picked up in church, that the more you give, the more you receive. That isn't why she gives, because she is really a very generous person. But the idea kind of appeals to me, and I hope she's right.

Ten

I read somewhere that men are by nature polygamous and that they were never meant to be tied to one woman all their adult life. Monogamy, this article said, is for the birds, and perhaps not even for them. This explains that Alec Guinness movie, if it needs any explaining, where he was a ship captain with a wife at each end of his run—one a comfortable British homebody and the other an exotic type given to off-the-shoulder blouses. Two wives, provided they are of such variety, would seem about the minimum to satisfy a man's needs.

Ever since I read this article and discovered it is only natural for a married man to look around, I have felt better about looking around.

Consider the situation on an airplane. Most passengers like a window seat where they can gaze at the scenery. *I* like an aisle seat where I can gaze at the stewardesses. Clouds are pretty, but stewardesses are prettier. Unlike clouds, they don't keep changing their shape every few minutes, and with the shape they have to start with, why should they? I have a lively imagination, but I have never imagined myself sitting close to a cloud, asking it where it came from and whether it likes to dance.

So I sit in an aisle seat and look at the kind of scenery I like best. And the scenery, which knows I am looking at it, looks back and smiles at me. Maybe laughs at me, considering my age and all that, but I prefer to think not. Perhaps it is the altitude, but when I am in a plane I forget about having almost no hair on top of my head and having a perfectly good wife at home (or, sometimes, with me). I get all sorts of romantic notions, especially after two Martinis and with that stereo music coming in through the earphones. As for those two Martinis, I drink very little at home or anywhere else—except on airplanes. I don't know why all this heavy drinking on planes, except for my general attitude, or altitude, of abandon. Feeling wicked, I let myself go.

My biggest thrill is when a pretty stewardess stops beside me, looks straight into my eyes, and says something very intimate and personal such as,

"Could I get you a magazine?" or, "Wouldn't you like a pillow?" The only trouble is that this shatters the beautiful dream I was having. But shortly thereafter I have another, and it is even better. In it, I am an airline pilot, a four-striper, and handsome in a rugged, mature way. All the women on the plane get goose pimples when I announce, after a glance at my altimeter, "We are now cruising at 37,000 feet." When I leave the plane, after maneuvering the huge jet to a perfect landing, I walk off with an adoring stewardess clinging to each arm.

I love the attention I get from stewardesses. The way, for instance, they bring me a box of chewing gum and hold it in front of me and trust me to take only one piece. Or the way they look to see whether my seat belt is fastened, as if they really care.

A woman who wants to please a man—either to get him or to keep him—should take a plane trip now and then and observe the stewardesses. Or a man can observe the stewardesses and make some helpful notes and give them to his wife. The notes might include such things as "Take off about fifteen pounds," "Take off about fifteen years," and "Bring me food and drink every hour or so." Some husbands may find it advisable to use a suggestion box and not sign their name.

The airlines do a marvelous job of selecting attractive stewardesses with an appealing seatside manner. But they could do a little more. In the pocket in the seat ahead of you, where they have all the flight charts and escape instructions and in-flight movie programs, they could include some additional information about the stewardesses aboard. As it is, all they tell you on the list of flight personnel posted just aft of the pilot's compartment is their names.

What I want in the little pocket in front of me, where I can take it out and study it, is something really helpful, like "Miss Sally Wentworth, 36–23–35, graduate of Wellesley, spent junior year in Paris, interested in modern art and music, designs her own dresses, has read all the latest books, cooks divinely, and has no steady boyfriend."

I am not just an old ogler. I am looking for a wife for my son. While he is casing the college campuses, I am scouting the airlines. Even if I don't find someone for him, I will have done my parental duty. Somehow, feeling I am doing something worthwhile, the trip seems shorter.

In some suburban communities, I understand, they have wife-swapping clubs. These must be interesting, but if there are any such in our town, we haven't been invited to join. With my luck, I would always get the worst of it, anyhow. And if my wife were swapping me, she would probably have to throw in something to boot, to make a deal.

A terrible thought comes to me. Perhaps my wife has been invited to join, as a singleton.

"We'll be glad to take you in," I can imagine the chairman of the membership committee telling my wife, "but we can't take that husband of yours. I'm sorry, but that's the way the club voted, unanimously."

I must drop in on that Wednesday Club of my wife's and see whether they really are all women, and whether they really do play bridge.

This brings me to the subject of jealousy. I don't see what is so bad about it. I think it is a great compliment when a wife is jealous of her husband. It shows she thinks he is attractive to other women. What I am leading up to is that my wife has never shown the slightest jealousy of me. I have had dozens of attractive women colleagues, considerably younger than my wife. I have had hundreds of beautiful students, several of them beauty queens. I have been with them, alone, in my office far into the night. I have been with them in the remote corners of the library stacks, ostensibly looking for a book. Never a word of suspicion or complaint from my wife. Indeed, if I should receive a perfumed letter, addressed to me in a feminine hand, and with "I

love you, I love you, I love you" written along the back flap of the envelope, she would probably lay it on my desk unopened and not even ask me about it.

It's a little discouraging.

As a matter of fact, my wife not only doesn't mind my looking at beautiful women, she points them out to me.

"Don't look now," she tells me in a restaurant, causing me to turn around immediately, "but there is a beautiful woman at the table behind you. My, I wish I had a figure like that."

After I have stared at this luscious creature about as long as I dare without getting punched in the eye by her escort, my wife finds me another one.

"Look over there, next to the man in the light suit. Isn't she gorgeous?"

I look, and she is. My wife has impeccable taste in picking out the beauties. She is as good as a man. We make a fine team, she picking them out and I looking.

If I were a hunter, I would take her along as my bird dog.

I always listen with awe and envy to married men who tell me of their conquests. It carries me back to the days when Carl Hawkins kept me posted. I don't care whether these men do all the things they say they do. I just like to listen. I never go to sleep the way I do at travel movies.

"There was this doll I met in the supermarket," they begin. "Boy, what a looker! Well, we got to talking, standing at the meat counter, and would you believe it. . . ."

I lean forward. My eyes bulge slightly. I try not to miss a word.

Another time I am fascinated is when a man who has been divorced a few times tells me about his previous wives. It's hard for me to imagine having been married more than once, and being able to compare.

I have a friend who has been married four times, and he is very generous in telling me about each of his wives. He feels a little sorry for me, with my limited knowledge.

"Tell me about your first wife again," I say.

"What do you want me to tell you this time?" he asks.

"Anything you think of," I say. "It's all very interesting."

It seems a little unfair, though. This friend of mine has to pay alimony, while I get the benefit of his wisdom free. I am learning so much about women from him, without running any risk myself, that I really should pay tuition.

But when you've had only one wife and never expect to have another, this is about the only way to enlarge your experience about matrimony.

Eleven

If so far in this account of my life with women I have seemed a Mr. Milquetoast, a dreamer instead of a doer, I must say categorically that this is not my fault. I put the blame on my father and grandfather, from whom I inherited the tendency. My father was not dominated by my mother, but he would do anything to avoid trouble, because my mother had ways of getting back at him. Her most effective way was the silent treatment, going around all day tight-lipped, without saying a word. Actually she rarely did this all day, because a couple of hours of it would usually bring my father to his knees.

"Say something," he would beg. "Say anything. I can't stand your damned silence any longer." He would then promise he would be good, and would never again do whatever he had done. My father was too fearful of my mother's retaliatory tactics to play around with other women, much as he may have wanted to.

But the one who really had no chance was my grandfather. He was cowed and as good as chained by my grandmother and spent most of his time in his third-floor hideaway. It was one place my grandmother never entered, but neither did any other women, because my grandmother sat where she could watch the stairway.

It all started with my grandfather, because his personal qualities and his experience or lack of experience with women influenced my father, and my father in turn influenced me. To understand me, you have to understand my grandfather.

My grandfather was a man of peace. And since he weighed only 130 pounds with his clothes on, it was just as well that he was not the belligerent type. The reason for my giving his weight with his clothes on rather than stripped is that he always weighed on the scales at the feed and fuel store, and with all those customers for feed and fuel standing around, no one was likely to weigh stripped—least of all my grandfather.

My grandfather was also lame. The reason he was lame was that when he was a child he was forbidden to walk along the top of a picket fence in the yard. He disobeyed and several times walked on the fence. Then one day he fell and was gored by a picket that entered the back of one knee. By the time he confessed to the disobedience and the accident, it was too late to remedy the damage he had done, and he was lame the rest of his life. My parents told me this story over and over, as a warning never to walk on a picket fence. But since I was afraid of high places, and we had no picket fence anyhow, the warning was unnecessary.

In addition to being lame and slight, my grandfather did not have the look of a pugilist. His eyes were large and brown and soft, and his mustache drooped weakly and sadly past the corners of his mouth. Many said he looked like Robert Louis Stevenson, though my grandfather looked as he did all the time, and not merely after a siege of tuberculosis.

My grandfather and grandmother (my grandmother outweighed my grandfather by fifty pounds, had a longer reach, and could have held her own in the ring) lived in Pomona, California, in a big house on the corner. Though they could not afford this three-story house with the longest, widest porch in town, it was what my grandmother wanted, and my grandfather simply worked longer hours. The longer hours were partly to pay for the house and partly to give my grandfather a reason for staying away from it. He was ill at ease with his big house and his big wife, both of which made him feel smaller by comparison. It was a house, too, in which my grandmother ran everything, including my grandfather. As the years went by, his big brown eyes looked sadder and sadder and his mustache drooped ever more dejectedly.

My grandfather's house was a considerable distance from the drugstore he operated downtown, but in spite of his lameness he always walked down

in the morning, back at noon for dinner (it was dinner at noon in those days), down again to the drugstore after dinner, back home for supper, down again to the drugstore in the evening, and home again after closing time. His were druggist's hours, not banker's. And though my grandfather and grandmother had a horse and buggy, it was inconceivable that he would drive to work. My grandmother had to have the horse and buggy to go to Women's Relief Corps or W.C.T.U. meetings.

Two blocks from my grandfather's house, on the way to his drugstore, they were building a new public library. Limping back and forth, on his way to and from work, my grandfather watched the progress of the building and passed the time of day with the contractor, Mr. Riley, who often stood out in front, supervising.

"Coming along nicely, isn't it?" my grandfather would say in his gentle, polite manner. Or, "Hope you get the roof on before the rains come."

Mr. Riley never said much. He was a man of few words but many pounds (about 225), with a red face, thick neck, and huge, rough hands. On rare occasions, melted down by my grandfather's warm smile, he would come out with something friendly, like "Howdy."

One thing troubled my grandfather about the construction of the library. There was usually a litter of planks, bricks, and strands of wire on the sidewalk, which more often than not was awash with water and leavings of wet cement. Lame as he was, walking was not easy for him under the best circumstances. With the sidewalk in this untidy condition, his footing was hazardous, and he had to pick his way carefully to keep from tripping or slipping. Several times he mildly mentioned the condition of the sidewalk to Mr. Riley.

"I have to watch my step here," he might say. Or, "I suppose you will be tidying this up before the weekend."

Mr. Riley would shift his cigar from one side of his mouth to the other and grunt in a way that my grandfather took to mean assent, or at least thinking it over. How was he to know that Mr. Riley took each comment on the condition of the sidewalk as a personal affront, that he had no intention of making any improvements for the sake of lame, busybody pedestrians, and that the fires of hatred were growing ever fiercer within him and one day must erupt with volcanic ferocity?

The day came.

Once again my grandfather made a kindly, half-playful remark as he picked his way over the debris on the sidewalk. Something like "It's a mite messier than usual today, isn't it?"

Perhaps it was the accumulation of such remarks. Perhaps it was something Mr. Riley had eaten from his dinner pail. At any rate, the volcano erupted.

Mr. Riley's red face suddenly became redder than ever and slightly purple across the forehead and around the eyes. Yanking his cigar from his mouth and throwing it to the ground, and lifting his huge fists in the manner of John L. Sullivan, he snarled at my grandfather, "Put up your dukes, and let's have it out here and now."

Quite possibly my grandfather failed to understand Mr. Riley's use of the word "dukes," thinking he referred to the husbands of duchesses. Or my grandfather may have been a little slow balling his hands into two pitifully small fists and getting them up between Mr. Riley and his jaw. Whatever the reason, his defensive measures were too little and too late.

One powerful blow from those massive fists, and my grandfather was wondering why it got dark so suddenly on a midsummer day. He was out cold, lying in the very debris about which he had complained, his head pillowed on a mound of wet cement.

I am not making this up. I read it in the files of our local newspaper of the year 1903. The headline screamed: E. E. ARMOUR ASSAULTED BY CONTRACTOR. LOCAL DRUGGIST KNOCKED UNCONSCIOUS. Perhaps at this point I should add that my grandfather's first name was Elmer, a poor name for a fighter, even a featherweight.

According to the newspaper, a crowd gathered and someone thoughtfully lifted my grandfather's head out of the wet cement, else he might have become part of the new library. Mr. Riley, a coward at heart, slunk away when no one was looking. My grandfather regained consciousness and was carried off, cement in his hair and shavings clinging to his coat, to the office of a nearby physician. A warrant was sworn out for Mr. Riley's arrest. A hearing was scheduled by the local judge for the next Tuesday.

I wish I could tell you how the hearings came out, and what happened to Mr. Riley. But though I looked at every item in the newspaper for the next several weeks, I found no further mention of the incident.

Knowing something of justice and of my grandfather, who was inclined to be unlucky, I can only hazard a guess about the aftermath of the Battle of the Sidewalk. My guess is that he was adjudged guilty of getting in the way of Mr. Riley's fist and forced to pay court costs and damages. The damages, of course, were entirely to my grandfather. It is unlikely, considering the softness of my grandfather's jaw, that Mr. Riley could have skinned his knuckles.

But regardless of the consequences, my grandfather had been in a fight. He had defended himself manfully, even though outweighed by nearly one hundred pounds. He had stood up (until he was knocked down) for clean sidewalks. Previously considered no more than an honest merchant, he was now regarded with new respect. There was talk of running him for mayor.

More important to my grandfather was the changed attitude of my grandmother. Overnight, she abdicated her position of dominance. She began to ask his opinion and defer to his judgment.

"Elmer," she said to him one day, "you might as well drive the horse and buggy to and from work. I can walk."

I learned an important lesson from the incident of my grandfather and the contractor. I learned that sometimes when you lose you win. And sympathy, leavened by a dash of respect, is akin to love.

Maybe my wife is so understanding of me, so lenient toward me, because she knows that I, like my grandfather, am a born loser, a gallant loser. It takes just the right kind of woman to appreciate this quality in a man, and fortunately, my wife is the right kind.

Twelve

Women may not be more irritable than men but they seem so, at least to men. Perhaps this is because they get tired more easily, and when they get tired the least little thing will upset them. Sometimes they give you warning, which is thoughtful of them.

"My nerves are in knots," my wife says, and I have a vision of synapses and dendrites all tied up in figure of eights, grannies, and assorted tangles. When she says her nerves are in knots I steer clear and say as little as possible and walk on my tiptoes.

I am also wary when my wife has a headache, especially when she has what she calls a "splitting" headache, which is the worst kind. Even when she has one of her lesser headaches, such as "a dull pain right here," I watch myself. It is no time to make disparaging remarks about her relatives or to criticize her way of keeping accounts.

Just as there are times when a woman is more jumpy than usual, there are certain subjects that are close to the nerve centers. Unless a man likes to live dangerously, he should let these subjects alone.

For instance, nothing is more certain to annoy my wife than for me to tell someone, especially a stranger, "My wife killed our dog." Since it is the truth, I really don't know why this should upset her, but it does. Her eyes narrow, her lips tighten, and, though she says nothing, you can see she is on the edge of an explosion.

The dog my wife killed was a shaggy white mongrel, part sheep dog and part no telling what else, named Happy. The reason he was named Happy was that he was always wagging his bushy tail and smiling. Maybe he wasn't exactly smiling, but the way his mouth opened and his eyes twinkled, everyone knew he was pleased with the way things were going.

He was happy with very little. When he followed me to my office at the college and I finally gave up yelling at him to go back and stopped throwing small stones at him (very gently), and let him come along, he was happy. When he wanted to go home and it wasn't time to go home but I couldn't stand his looking up at me with those big brown eyes and pawing at my pant leg and I said, "All right, let's go home," he was happy. When I cut his fur close with a pair of old shears, in the early days of summer, and didn't nip his skin as much as usual, he was happy. Most people require a great deal more to be happy than Happy.

Though we spoke of Happy as *our* dog, he was

really *my* dog. I did everything for him, and he knew it. I fed him and gave him water and washed him and picked the cockleburs out of his long white hair. He repaid me by following me everywhere, especially when I told him to stay home.

I did everything for Happy but kill him. My wife did that, as I have said—and as she thinks I have said too often. In most families someone else kills your dog, if your dog is killed. But we are a do-it-yourself family. We even killed our own dog. That is, my wife did.

Of course there were extenuating circumstances, as my wife keeps saying. She didn't know Happy was right behind the car when she was backing up. She didn't run over him on purpose. She liked Happy as much as anybody. And she didn't really kill him. When she felt something under the back wheel and heard Happy yelp, she stopped the car at once, and she saw Happy run up onto the lawn and lie down. Happy was still alive when she took him to the vet. It was the vet who killed him or, as he said, "put him to sleep," and maybe I should blame the vet.

I wasn't there, fortunately. I didn't see my wife run over Happy and I didn't see the vet do whatever he did. It is probably just as well I wasn't there, because the scene would haunt me. I am haunted enough, as it is, by what I imagine the scene to have been in the street in front of our house and in the vet's office.

Of course had I been there, things would have been different. "You might have run over Happy yourself," my wife says, and this gets under my skin about as much as what I say about what she did to Happy gets under hers.

That's about the way things stand, except that out of consideration for her feelings and to avoid those ugly looks she gives me (she can give some mighty ugly looks for a pretty woman), I have changed my story a little. Instead of saying, "My wife killed our dog," I say, "My wife ran over our dog." She thinks this sounds better, and perhaps it does. I shall try to remember to say it this way, because I really love my wife, even if she did kill Happy.

Another subject on which my wife is pretty sensitive is our children, or my attitude toward our children.

"You are too easy on them," she says. "You help them too much. They will never be able to do anything for themselves. They will grow up to be weaklings, and it will be all your fault."

"But," I say, "my father and mother never helped me much, and *I* grew up to be a weakling, didn't I?"

"That's true," she says, "but our children are

going to live in a more competitive society, where a person has to have some spine. You were lucky to grow up when you did. Just because you got by, don't think they can. Times have changed."

As you will see from the above, I blunt my wife's arguments by agreeing with her. I may go right on being easy on our children, but at least I don't annoy her by taking issue on some minor point, such as my personal character.

Where I have real expertise is in taking the blame. This is hard for anyone to do at first, but with practice it becomes fairly easy. I have got so I take the blame not only for things I have done but for things I have not done. Let us say, for instance, that my wife has burned a nasty place on her wrist by reaching into the oven to get a baked potato. While she is grimacing with pain and daubing the burn with butter, I stand by making helpful comments.

"It's my fault," I say. "I should have warned you to be careful." Or "I should have got the potato out myself." Or "I should have told you to fix boiled potatoes tonight, then this would never have happened."

Sometimes my wife thinks I demean myself a little too much, for example when I have done something wrong, such as forgetting to pick up the cleaning on the way home, and am a trifle theatrical in asking her forgiveness.

"I'll never forget to pick up the cleaning again, I promise, I promise, I promise," I say. While I am saying "I promise," I am on the floor, crawling toward her on my hands and knees, my head hanging penitently. Or I may hand her a golf club and say, "Beat me, right over the top of the head. Make a good scar, so when I look at myself in the mirror I'll remember not to forget."

This is little enough to do to avoid a quarrel. I would do even more if necessary.

The reason I am so eager to avoid a quarrel is that my wife occasionally uses the method my mother found so effective in dealing with my father, the silent method. In fact my mother may have coached her, she does it so well. How I wish she would scream at me, the way most men's wives do. At first I thought it was lack of vocabulary and bought her a dictionary of invectives, but she knew better than to fall for this.

I think the silent method, the quickest way to reduce a man to a quivering hulk, is inhuman. I think it should be outlawed, like genocide. The only good thing about it, I have discovered, is the wonderful sound of my wife's voice, no matter what she is saying, after a few hours of utter silence. A brilliant idea suddenly comes to me. Why not tape some of my wife's chatter and play it back the next time she tries the silent treatment on me?

I think I have found my secret weapon.

Until recently, I thought it wise to avoid quarrels with my wife at any cost, and I had been advising my friends to do the same. But now I am not so sure. Recently I read an article that makes me wonder. "A psychotherapist," says this article, "compares fighting between husbands and wives to a boxing match, and says it is a natural activity in healthy marital relationships." Let me conclude this chapter by enlarging on the psychotherapist's view:

From this, it suddenly appears
A marriage goes by rounds, not years,
And what is more, a good clean fight
With jabbing left and looping right
Is healthful. So don't give an inch,
Slug toe-to-toe. And in a clinch
 (Mistaken for a loving hug)
Get in some blows like any pug.

Ah yes, in marriage there is sparring
And now and then a jab that's jarring,
And fancy footwork, feints evasive,
And cuts, and wearing down abrasive,
Mismatches, all the rest, and yet
There's this of marriage, don't forget:
In this one sport of blows and shoves
The two contestants don't wear gloves.

Call me a coward if you wish, but with no ref-
eree and no attending physician, I'm not getting
into the ring. Or if I'm in the ring already, my
dukes are down. I'm not starting anything. Like my
grandfather, I'm a man of peace.

Thirteen

My wife is a great one for going to cocktail parties, and I go along because she says I must.

"You need to get out and see people," she says, without ever giving me one good reason why.

She has determined (and she is a very determined woman) that if we give two big cocktail parties a year, plus a couple of small, informal cocktail parties a month, this should be enough to keep us from being thought antisocial. "And you wouldn't want to be thought antisocial, would you?" she asks. I am still studying my answer.

Since going to cocktail parties occupies such a large part of my life, I have become somewhat of an authority on procedures, and I am happy to pass along information which may be helpful.

One of the crucial questions at a cocktail party is whether to eat so little as not to spoil your appetite for dinner or to eat so much that you can get by without having any dinner. The decision to eat little may, of course, be helped by there being little to eat. If, however, there is a large supply of tempting food, and your will power is a bit on the weak

side, one or more of several carefully developed techniques may be useful.

One way to keep from eating too much is to drink too much. If you keep your glass constantly at your lips, you will find it almost impossible to get food in. Furthermore, you will have to be moving back toward the bar a few minutes after leaving it if you are to get a refill and not be elbowed out of position, winding up with an empty glass in your hand. Also, after you have drunk enough you will lose all desire for food as well as your ability to walk to the table of hors d'oeuvres or, if you get there, to focus on anything or pick it up. And if you pass out completely, you won't eat a bite from that moment until you wake up at home, your wife looking into your face with loving concern and saying, "Well, you certainly made a fool of yourself."

Another way to keep from eating too much is to get into a lengthy argument over politics or movies or sex. (The last is a hard subject to get into an argument about, but interesting nonetheless.) You may have a deviled egg in your hand, but be so busy gesticulating with it as you make your point that you not only fail to get it into your mouth but let the stuffing fall out, and it takes a while to clean up the mess from the carpet.

"Think nothing of it," your hostess says, a look of horror on her face as she runs to the kitchen for a rag and a bottle of cleaning fluid.

Still another way is to keep distant from the enticing table by inviting one of the guests to accompany you on a tour of the garden. If the guest who goes with you is a beautiful young thing in a friendly mood after a couple of Martinis, and it is none too well lighted out there and you have to hold her around the waist to keep her from tripping, you may forget all about the lobster and the cold beef and the pineapple chunks. You may even forget about your wife, except to glance through the window and see that she is still there by the table, nibbling a piece of celery.

On the other hand, let's say you decide not to

avoid food, for fear of spoiling your appetite for dinner, but to eat so much that dinner will be unnecessary. This would seem to be easy, assuming there is a plentiful supply of tasty viands, but it isn't. I almost always choose the eat-enough-to-make-dinner-unnecessary alternative, because I know the food is better than anything I would get at home. So I have developed certain tactics and skills.

As soon as I have shaken hands with the host and hostess and made a few humorous remarks such as, "Good to be here," and "Happy to see you," I go in search of food. While others socialize, standing around with glasses in their hands (not to have a glass in your hand is to be thought a spoilsport, or one of the help), I head straight for the table on which are the goodies. A quick glance tells me whether there are only a few tidbits or the makings of a meal. If the latter is the case, I try to hide my elation. If I impulsively clap my hands, I do so quietly and unobtrusively. Now to eat.

But it is not so simple as that. Just as I am about to reach for a shrimp, my toothpick poised like a rapier, someone claps me on the back.

"Can't keep away from the food, eh?" says a friend, or erstwhile friend, wittily.

I am annoyed but relieved. It might have been my hostess, saying something to make me feel at home, such as "Go easy on those. I didn't expect so many to come to my party." Or "Are the shrimp all right? I was a little worried about leaving them out of the refrigerator so long."

Anyhow, I am slightly unnerved and drop the toothpick into the shrimp sauce. Shall I leave it there, floating on the top, try to fish it out, or push it below the surface where no one will be the wiser? It is an exciting experience, a moment of truth, calling for a clear head and a steady hand. Under such stress I have been known to drop my plate, thereby creating a diversion. Or I might nudge the guest ahead of me and whisper, "Hey, you left your toothpick in the shrimp sauce!"

Mostly, though, I just shuffle around the table, filling my plate and at the same time eating. This is important. Most people merely fill their plates. But I, more provident, eat as I go. Not to be thought greedy, I explain this by saying that I have to sample things first, to see whether I should take any.

"Very tasty," I say, standing over a clam dip into which I have dipped a cracker which I then plop into my mouth. "Very tasty indeed. I think I'll take some of that." So I dip three more crackers into the dip and put them on my plate. Before I move on to the next item, I half immerse another cracker (one for the road), which I munch as I move slowly and reluctantly on. Now I begin to look, with the cool appraisal of a professional, at what lies ahead.

The next dish is a bowl of olives. I take several, disdaining the spoon lying alongside. It seems to me silly that I cannot touch with my own hands the olives I am going to eat myself. Besides, no one is looking. As I transfer a few more olives to my plate, I survey the room to see where I can stow the pits. I am forehanded this way, always planning ahead. Noting several ashtrays, flower pots, and easily lifted throw rugs, I feel quite at ease on this score. No problem. Already, standing over the dish, I have eaten three olives, and have deftly placed the three pits in the trouser cuff of the gentleman in line ahead of me.

Another vexation is toothpicks. By the time I have used them to stab shrimp, lobster, cubes of cheese, and slices of pickle, I have quite a stack of many-colored picks. Unless disposed of soon, they will give people the impression that I am a glutton. Toothpicks, lighter and more likely to be caught by a gust of air, cannot be tossed so easily and accurately as olive pits. I have found the best temporary hiding place for used picks to be the lining of my coat. I weave them into the cloth with a couple of quick twists. It takes only a few minutes to remove them when I get home. They can be used over again, too. The only time I have been embarrassed was when I forgot to remove these party picks and sent my coat to the cleaner. When my coat came back it was accompanied by an envelope with my name on it. The picks were in the envelope. Cleaners are very honest men.

Some people wonder where to go with their plate of food after leaving the table. Into the next room? Into the garden? Shall they join old friends? Shall they try to get acquainted with people they have not met before?

I have no such problem. I don't leave the table. I just keep going around and around, eating as I go and replenishing my plate. If I don't go around very fast, it's because I don't want to get dizzy.

Finally my wife comes for me.

"Let's go," she says. "The party was from four to six, and it's quarter to seven now."

"Just one more shrimp," I say.

"You'll spoil your dinner," she says.

"Didn't you spoil yours?" I ask.

"No," she says. "Got talking."

That's the way it goes. We're always getting our signals mixed.

Fourteen

When my wife goes shopping for a new dress, I go with her. I suppose my main reason for accompanying my wife is the forlorn hope that I may persuade her not to buy anything.

"How do you like this one?" she asks, pirouetting in front of me.

"It doesn't *do* anything for you," I say. I have discovered that a dress must *do* something other than cover a woman's body. This seems a good deal to expect of a piece of cloth, but that's the way it is.

"Now, is this one any better?" my wife asks, modeling another.

"Maybe a little," I say. "Turn around and let me see the back." After she has turned around and I have been silent a moment, as if thinking, I come out with my crusher. "In back," I say, "it makes you look as if you had put on ten pounds, and all in one place."

While I am shrewdly torpedoing each dress, the salesgirl is trying to salvage a sale.

"It looks stunning on you," she says. "The color matches your eyes."

"It doesn't seem to hang quite right," I counter.

"We can fix that easily," the girl says, "by taking it in a little here."

"You know what happens when they start messing around," I say, growing a little desperate. "It'll never be right."

Sometimes the salesgirl wins, sometimes I do. We are pretty evenly matched. She has had more experience with women generally, but I know my wife better.

Often I ask to go into the little room with my wife, while she is trying on dresses, to save her coming out each time to show me. This way, too, I can get in some remarks about a dress the moment my wife has put it on, before the salesgirl has a chance. Perhaps that is why the salesgirl tries to keep me out.

"It might be better if you were to sit out here," she says, handing me a magazine. "The dressing room is small and a little stuffy." The way she looks at me, she makes me feel as if I'm trying to do something immoral, like force my way into the powder room, looking for powder. At least she suspects me of getting a kick out of watching my wife undress. More likely, she thinks this isn't my wife.

"My *wife*," I say, looking her straight in the eye

and being very firm about it, "needs me to zip her up."

So I walk past several dressing rooms where women are trying on dresses and, luckily, the doors are ajar. This enables me to look into each one to be sure my wife is not there. Finally, after a few false starts, I find my wife. I have to confess that I feel a little emotional about the whole business, and sometimes my mind wanders and before I know it my wife has bought a dress.

I never go with my wife when she is shopping for a hat. I know there is no stopping her. If she wants a

new hat, she will buy one. Unlike a dress, it will do no good for me to tell her it doesn't fit. Hats don't fit, they just sit. I'm not even sure whether they come in sizes, and if they do I don't see why.

One thing I know about hats. I wish my wife would keep her old one. I vaguely remember how outrageous I thought it looked when she bought it, but now I've grown accustomed to it. In fact I don't even notice whether she has it on or not, which is the best thing you can say about a woman's hat.

When my wife comes home with a new hat, I've learned not to make jokes about it. If there were any chance that by making scathing remarks I could turn her against her new hat and get her to take it back, I would make scathing remarks. But there is no chance whatsoever. Before I was absolutely certain about this, I used to try.

"Don't you think it's becoming?" my wife would ask, taking the new hat out of its box and placing it on her head.

"Becoming what?" I would come back sardonically.

"This is the very latest," she would say.

"It's later than you think," I would say. "Whoever designed that has been reading too much space fiction."

I had a number of ripostes almost as devastating as these, but I use them no longer. Now I simply ask some such searching question as "You're sure you won't be embarrassed?" or "How much?"

Moving down to the other end of my wife, I should like to make a comment on her shoes. In verse, it goes this way:

My wife has high-heeled shoes and low,
As you would think by now I'd know,
But still, when she's worn high-heeled shoes
And changes into low, it's news.
For suddenly my wife's so sunken,
So very short and small and shrunken,
That I look down and, on my soul,
Fear she has fallen in a hole.
Then, just when I'm adjusted to
Her smallness, she trades shoe for shoe,
And up she comes—we're neck and neck.
No wonder I'm a nervous wreck.

The only thing more ridiculous than stiletto heels on women's shoes is stiletto toes, which I am relieved to learn are no longer fashionable. I have seen my wife's feet, and I would swear that there are five toes on each foot—a big toe, a little toe, and three toes in between. There is a span of at least three inches from her big toe to her little toe, which I think is about normal. Yet she managed to crowd those three inches of toes into a shoe which, at the point, was less than half an inch across. This is not guesswork. I made a scientific study with a tape measure.

I honestly don't know how a woman got her toes

into those pointed shoes, unless the toes were all piled up, one on top of the other. I could find out, I suppose, with an X-ray or a fluoroscope, but it's a sight I would as soon not see. At any rate I can understand why, even wearing less extreme styles, a woman kicks off her shoes at the first opportunity.

One of my most embarrassing experiences was the time my wife took off her shoes during a movie. When the movie had got to the point where I whispered to her, "This is where we came in," she couldn't find one shoe. She groped around on the floor near her seat, and I groped around, but no luck. Finally I got down on my hands and knees and reached under the seat in front of my wife.

"I've got it," I whispered to her, handing her the shoe I had retrieved.

"Thanks," she whispered back. Then, a moment later, "It isn't mine."

I pushed the shoe back where I had found it and groped some more. After a bit, I got a firm hold on a shoe and thought I had it for sure this time, but a lady's foot was still in it. I gave up.

We sat there, my wife with one shoe on, until we had seen the movie through again and the lights came up for the intermission. Working fast, while the house lights were up and many patrons had left their seats to buy popcorn, I searched down toward the front from row to row.

"Pardon me," I said as I went along. "My wife has lost a shoe, a 7½AA. Have you seen it or felt it?"

I would like to tell you I finally found that shoe, but I didn't. The lights went off, the popcorn buyers came back to their seats, and I returned to my wife empty handed, except for a little popcorn a sympathetic fellow had given me.

"No luck," I said. "Are you sure you were wearing two shoes when you came?"

Rather than sit through the double feature again, we left. To facilitate walking, my wife took off her remaining shoe and padded up the aisle and out of the theater in her stocking feet. People were too busy watching the movie to pay any attention, but she got some curious stares as we walked the two blocks to where we had left the car parked.

The incident of my wife's shoes reminds me of women's gloves and some lines I once wrote on that painful subject:

> If men can buy suits
> With two pairs of pants,
> Then women, it seems,
> Should be given a chance
>
> To purchase three gloves
> At a slight extra cost—
> Two to be worn
> And one to be lost.

One simple solution to this whole clothing problem would be to join a nudist colony. At least then, when we were invited to a party and my wife said, "I haven't a thing to wear," I could reply, "Fine. Let's go. I'll be undressed in a jiffy."

Fifteen

My wife has never been able to balance her check-book. But then, neither have I. Each month when we get our bank statement we go through the same routine.

"The bank is off $16.40," she says. It is always the bank that is off.

"In our favor or against us?" I ask, this being my most penetrating question in the field of finance. If my wife says, "In our favor," I relax and think nothing more of it. If she says, "Against us," I fly into a rage.

"It's those new computers they're using," I say. "I don't trust them. You can't turn over everything to machines. Some gadget probably slipped a cog, and there goes our $16.40."

"Do you think one of the employees could be dishonest," my wife asks, "maybe taking a little out of each account and hoping nobody will notice?"

I know the very person my wife is thinking of, a young fellow who is too good-looking and too well-dressed to be working in a bank.

"I wouldn't put it past him," I say. "He couldn't own a car like that yellow convertible on his salary." I don't know what his salary is, and for all I know his wife is loaded, but at a time like this I usually think the worst of people. My wife has cranked up my imagination and I am off. In my mind's eye I see this embezzler in some Latin-American country with which we have no extradition treaty, sitting in a fancy cocktail lounge with a beautiful *señorita* on either side of him. He is buying them drinks—with *our* money.

Sometimes my wife and I go storming into the bank, demanding that the error in our account be rectified. Or, to put it another way, that the money that has been swindled from us be put back. It takes someone high up, the manager or at least the assistant manager, to convince us that we have made a simple mistake in addition or, more likely, in subtraction, subtraction being harder for both of us. I can take $124 from $368 without too much difficulty, but taking $659 from $837, when I have to start right out by taking 9 from 7, is beyond me mathematically.

We leave the bank convinced, or partly convinced, that an honest error has been made, and even that it was we who made it. If a little suspicion lingers, it is because we find it hard to see how *everybody* in the bank can be honest, with all that money lying around. What further undermines our confidence is our catching a glimpse of that too-good-looking, too-well-dressed employee. There is something shifty about his eyes, something weak about his chin. If it weren't for our liking the color of the checks at this bank better than the color of the checks at the bank in the next block, we would pull out every cent. That would show them.

Sometimes, as I say, my wife and I go into the bank together, to complain about an error in our checking account. More often, though, I go to the bank by myself. I have another reason for going, and I don't need my wife. In fact I don't want her along.

On these occasions, frankly, I go to the bank because I need a boost to my ego. In my hands is a sheaf of important-looking papers. There is an intense, purposeful look on my face. The bank manager, sitting at a large desk with his nameplate on it and discussing a loan with a client, looks up and smiles at me. For all he knows, I am coming in to make a deposit.

The assistant manager also stops whatever he is doing to nod cheerily at me. He knows me well, ever since I accused the bank of making an error in my account and he had to explain to me that $298 and $126 are $424. I must have carried over the wrong number, not being used to such large amounts.

The first teller, a blonde, waves to me as I pass,

her hand fetchingly full of greenbacks. So does the second teller, a brunette. So does the third teller, a redhead. In hiring tellers, the bank's policy is to please everyone. Competition is pretty keen in the banking business these days, and the savings and loans have snapped up some of the best lookers.

But I stop at none of the tellers' windows. Nor do I go to one of the center tables to fill my fountain pen, now that the bank has converted to ball point pens and these are attached to a chain which, if you exert too much force on it, sets off the burglar alarm. I may take a quick peek at each of the tables to see whether anyone has left any cash, the way I flip open the coin return box on pay telephones. But this is not the primary purpose of my visit. I have more important business at hand.

Finally I come to the young lady just beyond the tellers' windows. Her hair is a nondescript color, but she was hired anyhow, in a moment of weakness. The weakness was on the part of the personnel manager, a young man who, glancing over her application blank, or form, noticed her measurements were 40–23–36. He thought she would do very well, standing sideways in the narrow entrance, blocking the way to the bank vault if anything should happen to the door.

But before I can enter the vault with this young lady, I must go through a certain routine, and I rather like it. First I sign the guest book, adding my

name to a long list of local celebrities, and after my
name the young lady writes the day and hour.
Then, like a member of some privileged group, say
a Playboy Club, I draw out the key to my safe
deposit box. There is a number on it, and the girl
checks this number against a number in a card file.
I am beginning to feel like James Bond, 007, going

through a little secret stuff with Pussy Galore, who ostensibly is working for the bank but really is on *my* side.

My nostrils flare, and her nostrils look a little dilated too.

"Shall we go into the vault?" she asks, looking straight into my eyes, as if plumbing their depths. Never have I seen a prettier plumber.

"Yes," I say forcefully, trying to impress on her that I am a man of few words and that this is not a time for speeches anyhow. I thoughtfully rub my cheek, hoping she will notice what a heavy masculine beard I have. It could hardly be five o'clock shadow, because the bank closes at three.

Once our two keys have been inserted in the box and the numbered door swings open, my fantasy changes. I am no longer the suave James Bond, 007, and the young lady is no longer Pussy Galore. I am J. Paul Getty, the richest man in the world, and the young lady with me is my private secretary.

"You may wait outside the vault," I say.

"As you wish, sir," she says.

She may be my private secretary, but there are a few things she will never know, such as whether I am worth $800,000,000 or $900,000,000. Some things I prefer to keep to myself. . . .

All the time I am thinking about the problems of being the richest man in the world, I am riffling through the contents of my safe deposit box. Finally

I place in the safe deposit box the sheaf of important papers I had brought in with me, and take out another sheaf of important papers. I may even take out the same sheaf of papers I put in.

At last I summon the young lady. As we place our matched keys in the box and lock it, my fantasy heats up again. Once more I am James Bond, and I imagine we are using our two keys, in an intimate way, to lock the back door of her apartment after a cozy evening together, and I wonder whether Security has kept a fix on me, thanks to the transistor in the hollowed-out heel of my shoe. It could have been a nasty bit of business, otherwise, if one of Goldfinger's agents had tossed some cyanide pellets into the vault and then slammed shut the massive door and left me there to die an agonizing death, clutching my millions. . . .

"Where have you been?" my wife asks when I get home.

Why does she always want to know where I've been? Can't a man even go to the bank now and then without being cross-examined?

"Just down town, looking around," I say. If I told her what I had been doing, and thinking, she wouldn't understand.

Or maybe she would.

Sixteen

A woman, I have discovered, gets out of shape awfully fast. A man marries a woman who wears a size ten, and in a year or so she is up to (or out to) a fourteen, and still going. You would think with all the housework she does, or claims to do, all the wielding of mops and brooms and lifting of laundry, she would keep trim. But after a few years she starts to sag, as if she is made of putty. What were once curves become bulges, and her husband sighs, as Wordsworth once did in another connection, "Oh, the difference to me!"

I have been determined that my wife would keep her figure, which was a very nice one to start with. After all, it was one of the things I married her for, one of the main things. I hate to see it go to pot.

Fortunately, my wife is almost as eager to keep her figure as I am for her to keep it, though for different reasons. She is motivated by personal pride, which is a good enough motivation if you haven't any other.

"I hope I don't get like that," she whispers to me,

nodding toward a woman who has begun to settle, in fact is beyond the beginning stage.

"You won't if you work at it," I whisper back, though I am not wholly convinced. I have seen too many women who, though they live on lettuce and skimmed milk and do all sorts of exercises, get fatter and fatter and more and more shapeless, the putty settling into a lump. But a good figure is worth putting up a fight for.

The trouble with my wife is that she has never been much of an athlete or sportswoman. She doesn't play golf or tennis. She doesn't hike. In fact she doesn't walk any farther than she has to. Sometimes, after I have maneuvered back and forth to wedge our car into a parking space, she spots a parking space twenty feet closer to where we are going and asks me to repark.

"It's these shoes," she says.

"What's the matter with them?" I ask.

"They're not my walking shoes," she says.

I thought all shoes were meant to walk in, but apparently not.

Even in her walking shoes, my wife rarely walks. About the only time she walks any distance is when she is shopping, trudging the hard sidewalk from store to store. The truly miraculous thing about this is that when she is shopping she does all this walking in her nonwalking shoes. The same shoes worn under any other conditions would have her moaning, "My feet are killing me," in a few minutes. There is something uncanny about this. It is a little like an Indian fakir walking on a plank of upturned nails or a bed of hot coals—either a trick or a mystic triumph of spirit over body.

However, shopping doesn't come under the category of exercise. At least it seems to do no good for a woman's figure. Indeed it seems to have the opposite effect, perhaps because of all the standing at counters, all the breathing of bad air in crowded elevators, all the eating of samples at the supermarket. Shopping may tire a woman, especially if she fails to find what she is looking for in her size, but it doesn't make her any slimmer at the waist.

For a while my wife got up early and did calisthenics in front of the TV, wearing a sheer nightgown. The muscular young man on TV told her what to do, such as put her hands on her hips and bend to this side and that side and forward and back and inhale and exhale, and he counted for her in a lusty baritone: "One, two, three, BEND, one, two, three, BEND." When he had finished each exercise, he chatted for a few minutes in a friendly way, getting off such pleasantries as "Now feel the muscles in your abdomen!" and "Don't you notice more firmness in the bust?"

I'll have to confess I got jealous of that fellow on TV with the big biceps, and my wife standing in front of him in her sheer nightgown.

"Hasn't he the most wonderful shoulders?" she made the mistake of saying.

"He splits infinitives," I sneered, trying to cut him down to my size. "And he misuses 'like.' "

"Notice those muscles in his forearms," she sighed, so fascinated she failed to hear me.

Though I disliked to stoop to anything so underhanded, and hated to deny myself some of my favorite programs, I finally disconnected a small wire in the TV set. It was two weeks before we could get a repairman to call. By that time, as I had hoped, my wife had got out of the habit of morning calisthenics.

I was no longer plagued by jealousy, but my wife, I could plainly see, was getting flabby. That TV instructor had helped her, no question. But there must be some other way.

There was. My wife started going to a woman who took off fat by means of rollers. She didn't really take it off, she moved it from one place to another. That was all right with me, because I have no objection to fat in the right areas. That is probably why I was so intrigued by the following news item I came upon recently: "When a man gives a woman his coat on a chilly day, according to a health expert, he is not just being gallant, he is being foolish, because the fat of a normal woman is thicker than that of a man and she tolerates cold better." I wrote the following lines on this subject:

Henceforth I'll keep my coat on
   When days are drear and chill.
It's something I shall gloat on,
   I'll not risk being ill.

Let girls think me bad mannered,
   Repulsive and uncouth.
I'll wear a coat that's bannered:
   "I'm not a silly youth,

I'm no Sir Walter Raleigh,
        No turner-on of charm.
My coat off would be folly,
        You've fat to keep you warm."

Or so I dream, R. Armour,
        Yet as one who observes
That fat that makes girls warmer
        Is also what makes curves,

I know that I'll de-coat me
        With one impulsive clutch
For someone who—just note me—
        Has fat, but not too much.

The woman who used rollers on my wife did it by means of machines on which my wife would lie or sit while the rollers did their work, like so many rolling pins flattening out cookie dough. I never saw the machines in operation, but my wife described them to me.

"Is there any chance of a malfunction?" I asked. I could imagine my wife accidentally getting between two rollers, like the wringers of a washing machine, and coming out paper thin.

"Oh, heavens no," she said. "They're perfectly safe." Once again she explained what they looked like and how they operated, but I never quite understood.

Anyhow, the rollers helped. They took inches off her waist and put them where they were more useful, or at least ornamental. My wife always came back from a session with color in her cheeks and a sparkle in her eyes. Some of this came from the rollers and some, I suspect, came from the rollees, women undergoing treatment at the same time as my wife and able and willing to talk despite (or perhaps because of) the pommeling. My wife had to pay for being rolled, but the gossip and spicy stories she picked up in the rolling parlor were free.

Had we not moved away, I suppose my wife would still be getting those workouts. But we moved to another city, where, though she looked in the yellow pages of the phone book, she could find no one with a roller franchise. She talked for a while of getting the name of the manufacturer and installing a set of rollers at home. But she could never figure out where. Our bedroom is too small, what with the beds and dressers, and rollers in our living room would clutter up the place, though they would make a stimulating conversation piece.

So it was that my wife finally came to the exercise on which she now depends to keep her figure from getting any worse. I can best express my first experience with it as follows:

> My wife does yoga every morning
> In leotards. I give you warning,

Should you come on her, clad in black,
Upon the floor upon her back

And writhing as in throes of death,
With rolling eyes and gasping breath,
You'd think her battling two black snakes
And cry out, "Oh, for goodness' sakes!"

I did this once, and I can tell you
I gave a scream, a frightened yell you
Could hear for blocks. Though now I wince,
I've not recovered fully since.

Until she learned the exercises and became a do-it-yourself yogi, she went to a class each week. There she joined about a dozen middle-aged women who writhed around on the floor together under the supervision of a professional. Startled as I was by my first glimpse of my wife's private sessions, I am sure my psyche would have been irreparably damaged at the sight of yoga on such a large scale —and a large scale would be necessary to weigh some of the behemoths in the group. Fortunately, I never came upon them unexpectedly, all simultaneously doing the abdominal power whip.

Yoga may or may not have improved my wife's figure, but it has done one thing for her for certain. It has made her limber. Lying down, she can bring her legs back over her shoulders until her toes touch the floor. In fact she can wrap her feet around the back of her head and look out to the rear as if she has been decapitated and her head has been set where it was never intended to be, like a Halloween pumpkin. I remember how, when I was a boy, I saw a contortionist do this in the circus and it made me sick.

It still does.

Seventeen

Now we are getting near the end, and I mean this in more ways than one.

My wife is convinced she is going to predecease me. I tell her this is nonsense. She is a healthy woman with only a little arthritis, and arthritis never killed anyone. It only makes her neck a little stiffer and thus harder for her to turn quickly when there is something interesting to see. I am sure she will outlive me by at least ten years, and I keep telling her so.

Which one of us will die first is about the only thing we quarrel about, since we are really quite happily married.

"I tell you *I* will," my wife says, after we have been arguing a while, her voice rising slightly and taking on volume.

"Don't be silly," I shout back, "*I* will."

I doubt that our neighbors can hear us, but if they can, they probably only wonder what we are at odds about—maybe money or my wife's relatives, they think, being as wrong about this as about most things. Their trouble is that they assume we are normal people, like themselves.

My wife has one statistic on her side. She is seven months older than I am. Nor is she reticent about this. Given half a chance she will explain that from her birthday, in December, to my birthday, in July, she is a year older than I am, and that we got married three days before her birthday so our marriage license would show us the same age. Three days later and she would seem to be marrying a man a whole year younger. Of course she *looks* younger than I do, as everyone tells her and she doesn't mind hearing.

When we are arguing about which of us will outlive the other, she always drags in the fact that she is older than I am.

"Just use your common sense," she says in a slow, quiet way, as if speaking to a child. "The older person is almost sure to go first."

I hate this "go first" business. For one thing, it brings up the question of where I am going, and, frankly, I don't know. For another, I have the urge to correct my wife by saying it isn't "men first," but "ladies first." However, this would play into her hands. I am trying to convince her that, at least in this instance, it is men who go first. And I have the statistics to prove it.

"Women live longer than men," I say, waving an actuarial table in her face. "If you don't believe

these figures, just look around at all the widows."

"But their husbands probably didn't take care of themselves the way you do."

By this she means that I do push-ups every morning. What makes no impression on her, even though I tell her over and over, is that I do fewer push-ups every year.

"And you haven't a sick bone in your body," she throws in as a clincher.

It's true my bones are healthy enough, but I have troubles more serious and more likely to carry me off than her arthritis. I catch cold more often than she does, and when I have a cold I feel worse. At least I think I feel worse, and so does everyone else, because I complain louder.

And I have terrible insomnia. I am wide awake all night. My wife says I must sleep a little, because she can hear me snoring. But I tell her she must be dreaming, or listening to herself. Besides, I snore when I am wide awake. It has something to do with a deviated septum in my nose, which could be fatal almost any time, especially if it cuts off my breathing completely.

"You come from a long-lived family" is another of her arguments.

"There was my Uncle Paul," I say to this one. "He died when he was thirty-two."

"He was run over," my wife says, "and that has nothing to do with your genes."

I shrug. You can't win them all.

It may seem silly that we should give each other such a bad time about longevity. I would be willing to yield, being a conciliatory sort, and say, "All right. Have it your own way. You will probably die first." But this would only set things up for my wife's favorite pastime.

I refer to her little game of picking a second wife for me.

"When I am gone," she starts out, with a misty look in her eyes—she means gone for good, not just away for a few days' visit with her sister—"I know you will marry again, and I think you should."

I never know whether to say of course I will or of course I won't. If I say of course I will, she might break down and cry and say, "You just want to get rid of me." (She watches Alfred Hitchcock movies and might get the idea I am poisoning her slowly, by slipping something into her coffee.) So I never say I will marry again. If that is what she wants me to say, to confirm her suspicions, I am too smart for her.

Nor do I say I won't. She has extrasensory perception and she knows when I am lying. So I say something noncommittal, such as, "Oh, lay off." Or I return to our original argument, saying, "What's the use of bringing that up again? You are going to outlive me, anyhow."

But no matter what I say, my wife persists in nominating her successor. Fortunately she can only nominate, not elect.

"I think Elinor would be just right for you," she says.

"That's absurd," I say. "You know she is taller than I am."

"Not in flats," she says. "In flats she is just about your height."

"Do you think she would wear flats to a dress-up party just so as not to tower over me? Anyhow her teeth stick out."

"You're making a mistake if you don't take Elinor," my wife says. "But if your mind is made up, how about Roberta? She would make you a wonderful wife."

"She's too fat," I say. "And besides, you know how we argue about politics. Frankly, I can't stand her."

"She's a marvelous cook."

"Maybe that's why she's so fat. No thanks, not Roberta."

And so my wife goes through the list she is always working on when she should be washing the windows or ironing my shirts. I know them all: Elinor, Roberta, Helen, Joan, and Virginia. Now and then she takes a couple of names off, but she always adds that many more.

Nancy is a recent addition. "I have just the one for you," my wife said one day. "She would make you a perfect wife."

"Who is that?" I asked, unable to conceal my curiosity, though prepared to scoff at the suggestion.

"Nancy," she said.

"You don't mean Nancy Perkins, do you? She giggles all the time. You know I don't like women who giggle."

"No," my wife said, "I mean Nancy Oliver."

"But what about Tom?" I asked. "You know Nancy is happily married."

"Yes, but Tom won't live forever."

"Will Nancy?"

"She'll outlive Tom."

"What makes you think so?"

"Tom is three years older. He's already had one heart attack. Besides, he doesn't get enough exercise."

"I wouldn't want to wait around until I was seventy, just on the chance," I said. "And I don't care for Nancy, anyhow. She has big legs."

"So you've been looking," my wife said.

"I can't keep my eyes closed all the time," I said. "Besides, it was just a quick look, and I didn't like what I saw."

When my wife and I have an argument like this, we shout back and forth at each other a little. But we are friends again as soon as one or the other of us walks out and slams the door and then comes back thirty seconds later and is sorry.

Not being a psychologist, I can't figure out why my wife persists in thinking up women for me to marry when she is gone. She may actually be worried about me, fearing I may marry the wrong person and be miserable, or not marry at all and be miserable. Or she may want my sympathy, about her dying so soon and all that. Or she may like to hear me say why I wouldn't marry this one or that one, either (1) reassured that I won't marry anyone else, which is what she secretly hopes, or (2) flattered, by comparison, when I say derogatory things about these other women that I don't say about her, which is the next best thing to being praised.

Anyhow, I seem to be doing the right thing in rejecting all of her candidates for a second wife. Each time she runs through her list and I find some reason why I could not be happy with Elinor, Roberta, Helen, Joan, Virginia, and Nancy, she seems a little happier or more confident or something.

One woman my wife suggested only once and has not mentioned since is Donna, a cute divorcée who, in my honest opinion (which I keep to myself), has everything. She is pretty, intelligent, charming, and loaded. The time my wife asked, "How about Donna?" I had to think fast. We agree on politics, her teeth are perfect, she doesn't giggle, and her figure is just right, including her legs.

"Donna who?" I asked, playing for time.

"Why, there's only one Donna. Donna Mayfield, of course. She is just the one for you."

"Oh, Donna," I said casually, as if I finally remembered who she was, not having thought of her in years. Actually I had seen her in the supermarket only last week in tight-fitting blue-and-white striped capris and had helped her carry her groceries to her car.

"Yes, Donna," my wife said, and I could imagine her extrasensory apparatus starting to mesh.

"Don't be ridiculous," I said. "She's too young for me. What do you think I am, a cradle robber?" I put on the expression of one shocked and scandalized at such an idea. I would have said, "I'm old enough to be her father," if I had thought of it. Actually I am only twenty years older than Donna, and just look at all those Hollywood stars marrying girls thirty or forty years younger.

It was the best I could do on short notice. My wife seemed to be satisfied. Anyhow, she scratched Donna's name off the list more quickly than some of the others. As I say, she never mentioned her again, and neither did I.

Sometimes I think my wife is hinting around for me to make up a list of men who might make her a good husband after I am gone. But it is hard for her to come right out and say so, having insisted all these years that she will go first. If this is her game, I won't play. Even without extrasensory perception I could tell which ones she would be pretty happy with. And I wouldn't like it.

So she can go on suggesting successors for herself if she wants to. And I'll go on telling her what is wrong with each one of them, even though it may be hard to think up something each time. It keeps me on my toes.

For her part, she can keep on insisting that she will go first. If she doesn't believe the statistics, she can look at all those widows.

As a matter of fact, I can look at all those widows too. Most men go first, but those who hold out have it made.

Eighteen

Here and there, in the chapters above, I have become so emotional on the subject of women and/or married life that I have lapsed into verse. The reader who does not care for verse will have recognized these lapses because the lines did not come out even on the right-hand side of the page, and he will have skipped them. Such a reader now has a treat in store for him. He may skip this entire chapter.

What follows is a small anthology of light verse about women and, especially, the husband-wife relationship. It may not be great poetry, but it scans.

THERE'S A CATCH TO IT

A member of the National Health Authority says he wishes he could hire more women as dog catchers, since they are more adept at it.—*News item.*

For creeping up on dogs, and pouncing,
For grabbing them, without announcing,
A woman's better than a man.
Those he can't catch, she will and can.

He may be quicker, may run faster,
May be a better dog-net caster,
But she, a woman sweet and charming,
Is much more subtle, more disarming.

A dog who sees a woman nearing
Will wag his tail, no danger fearing,
Will hear her words, will like the tone,
Will think: "She's bringing me a bone."

Not till too late will he discover
That she's no friend at all, no lover,
But someone sent, by gad, to get him
And, when he's not suspecting, net him.

CLOSETED

My wife and I have two closets
   We share to the best of our powers.
One closet is strictly for *her* clothes,
   The other is strictly for *ours*.

LEAVE ME YOUR NUMBER AND I'LL HAVE HER CALL YOU

My wife, and I don't mean to wrong her,
Is really quite a Big Belonger.
Indeed, she's joined some real humdingers:
Assorted groups of doorbell ringers,
Collecting for all kinds of causes
(They rarely give the doorbell pauses),
As well as clubs of culture seekers
That listen blissfully to speakers,
And groups that have a weekly meeting
For exercise, topped off by eating,
And circles which, as I have noted
To bridge and gossip are devoted. . . .
At times, when eating by my lonesome,
At suchlike times, and I have known some,
I say of this Belonger: she
Belongs to everything but me.

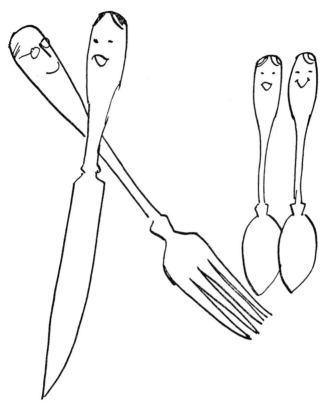

TOGETHERNESS

A man and his wife
Are like fork and knife
And they live together in clover
If she, being sharp,
Doesn't cut and carp
Too much, and if he forks over.

FURNITURE DERANGEMENT

Is our living-room furniture strangely arranged?
  Do you wonder just why things are there,
At such an odd angle—
A kind of a tangle—
  That sofa, that table, that chair?

It isn't for beauty, it isn't for style,
  It's not that it's comfy and snug,
But thus we are able,
With chair, sofa, table,
  To cover three spots in the rug.

TELL THEM THE ONE ABOUT

When I'm telling a story, my dear, loving wife
Cuts in. (When she cuts, she's as sharp as a knife.)
She says, "It was Plinkton, not Plimpton, remember?
And it happened in August, I'm sure, not
      September."
She lets me proceed for a minute, or nearly,
Then says, "On the *left,* I recall it quite clearly."
Do I maybe get back at my wife when she's telling
A story and spoil it just as it is jelling?
No, I don't, and the reason is this, in a line:
She doesn't tell stories, she'd rather wreck mine.

HEARING ISN'T BELIEVING

A housewife calls her husband
    From workshop, yard, or den
When dinner's on the table,
    And calls him once again.

She's glad, of course, on hearing
  . At last that voice of his,
But also knows "I'm coming"
    Doesn't mean he is.

CO-PILOT

Some women are backseat drivers
And, sitting alert in the rear,
Wherever they go
Give out with a flow
Of cautions their husbands can hear.

No backseat driver is *my* wife,
She's a different model and make.
She sits alongside
Where the speed may be eyed,
And her foot hovers close to the brake.

SUNDAY SUPPER

At home Sunday nights, it's each man for himself
As we open the cupboard and ogle the shelf
And whiff at the leftovers, test with our thumbs,
And spread stuff on crackers and scatter the crumbs.

We jimmy a jar and we empty a bottle,
We finish up foodstuffs before they can mottle.
We eat what we want, what we can, what is canned,
What we find, what we fix, and far more than we
planned.

ASHES TO ASHES

Housewives go into a horrible passion
On finding an ashtray that has a small ash in.
You drop in an ash and you puff until ready
To drop in another—then careful, friend, steady.
The ashtray is gone, being emptied and polished
Till every last trace of the ash is abolished.

Ah, there it is, back once again on the table.
Now drop in your ash, and then wait, if you're able,
While once more it's emptied and scoured and made
    shiny
And there isn't a trace of an ash, even tiny.

A woman will fill up an ashtray with pins
And needles and buttons and suchlike. The sin's
When a man, stupid fellow, so foolish and rash is
As to think that an ashtray's intended for ashes.

INCOMPETENT

My wife insists, with weary sigh,
I do not wipe the dishes dry.
She says I merely make some passes
And leave large spots upon the glasses.
Or, when I take the wash routine,
She says I do not get things clean.

You'd think, when I do things so ill,
She very soon would have her fill
And send me packing, useless bum,
Back to the book she dragged me from.
But though I drive her nearly mad,
Apparently I'm not *that* bad.

LET'S FACE IT

Sometimes when my wife
Says, "I look a sight,"
I say, "Dear, of course not,"
But really she's right.

IN THE BAG

This I must say of ladies' handbags:
They have become such huge and grand bags
That what was once a dainty, cute case
Is now more like a full-sized suitcase.
And in the future, sure as fate,
As handbags grow in size and weight,
So women's muscles will develop
Till men, too late, will cry for helop.

FORGIVE ME, CAT LOVERS

Dogs are increasing in popularity as pets, while cats are declining, and kept mostly by women.—*News item.*

I do not wonder cats are less
And less in favor, and can guess
The reason they're of late declining,
And I'm, I must confess, not pining.

Consider playing with a cat.
Will it fetch sticks and such as that,
Stand on hind legs and, while you boss it,
Catch in its mouth the food you toss it?

Or take a walk. See how it feels
To have a cat tag at your heels.
It won't tag long—some dog will send it
Up tree or pole, and that will end it.

Some women, though, still make a beeline
For every scrawny, mangy feline,
And love to keep and feed and carry one.
I'm only glad I didn't marry one.

WHY DOESN'T SHE TELL ME?

When we have dinner guests, my wife
Will sometimes give me looks
That have the sharpness of a knife,
The barbs of fishing hooks.

And why the awful inward throes
With which she nearly bursts?
I've offered seconds, and *she* knows
That there are only firsts.

BUDGETARY PINCH

Although we twist and nudge a bit,
Our budget doesn't budge a bit,
Which makes us, you can judge, a bit
    Upset, and causes cries.
It worries and incenses us,
It isn't half immense as us,
It cabins, cribs, and fences us—
    We need a larger size.

NOOK KNACK

We have a breakfast nook in which
We breakfast. It is just a niche,
And getting in requires finesse,
And getting out, I'd say, no less.
Indeed (and this I must deplore),
Once we have eaten, it takes more.
Oh well, our breakfast nook, no beauty,
Serves well, in fact does double duty:
It's there we eat and, sitting, rising,
It's there we do our exercising.

SEE HERE, BUD

My wife will sometimes work for hours
Arranging, rearranging flowers
And picking out the proper vase
And moving it from place to place.

You'd think the posies would be grateful
For all this care. But they are hateful.
For, once they're fixed, moved hither, thither,
They hide their little heads and wither.

COO COO

Doves without mates coo ten times as much as doves with mates.—*News item.*

Hark, hark the single dove that coos,
And as he softly coos he woos.
For female doves that flock around
Are fascinated by the sound.
It is so hearty and so hale,
So very lovely, dovely male.

But once a male dove finds a mate,
His coos quite suddenly abate.
In fact the drop in coos is such
He only coos a tenth as much
And mostly, I am forced to say,
In a subdued, self-conscious way.

Oh, there are times he has the urge
And stops himself, right on the verge,
Or if he's just a bit too late
And starts to coo, then sees his mate,
He flies down from the perch above
And says, "I coo for you, my dove!"

IT'LL BE A BEAUTY

My wife has a dressing-room table that's filled
With all sorts of items with which she is skilled:
With creams that are cleansing and creams that are
    vanishing,
With potions for adding and lotions for banishing,
With curlers and tweezers and clippers and files,
With bottles and boxes and hairpins in piles.
It looks, I confess, like a chemistry lab,
This place where for hours she can dibble and dab,
And I hope she knows well what it says on each label
That graces the bottles and jars on this table,
Or some day, at work here combating erosion,
She'll leave us, I fear, in a mighty explosion.

MAN OF MUSCLES

Yes, I unscrew the tops from jars,
Although they stick their worst,
And get admiring glances from
My wife, who with her tiny thumb
Has got them loosened first.

OVERSTATEMENT

My wife exaggerates quite a lot.
   The thought of it rankles and lingers.
She says I'm all thumbs. I insist that I'm not—
   Just my fingers.

STEP RIGHT UP

My wife and I aren't showy, vain folk,
We're cautious people, safe-and-sane folk.
So when there's need around our house
To mount a ladder, my good spouse
And I, with care and well-planned scheme, work
Together in long-practiced teamwork.
To make quite certain nothing's wrong,
We check each step, make sure it's strong,
And level legs so they are steady.
At last, when everything is ready,
Since I know how, a skilled old-timer,
I hold the ladder—she's the climber.

ROMANTIC YARN

They say we're a close-knit family,
And the term is a term that fits.
For I, I'll admit, am close,
And my wife—well, my good wife knits.

LET THAT HOUSEKEEPING KEEP

Lay that dust rag down, dear,
  Put aside your mop.
Can't you see my frown, dear?
  Please, my darling, stop.

Cut the vacuum cleaner,
  Let the broom be gone.
(Also you look leaner
  With your girdle on.)

Work to make things spic, sweet,
  Shine the brass and chrome.
Stop it, though, and quick, sweet,
  Now that I am home!

SHEAR NONSENSE

Surveys show that the most-used kitchen utensil is not the
coffee pot or the bread knife but the kitchen shears.—*News
item.*

Come, let us hymn the kitchen shears,
Most used of all, it now appears:
The shears that clip, the blades that whack
A piece of string, a balky sack,
A bit of foil, a hunk of rag—
And never droop and never sag.

These shears, though seeming frail and thin,
Are also used for cutting tin,
For lifting out a stubborn cork
That wouldn't yield to pick or fork,
For prying up a lid, tight stuck,
That comes with muscles and with luck.

Shears can, in fact, have many uses,
Like stirring paints and mixing juices,
Or hammering a good-sized nail.
Whatever need, shears seldom fail.
That's why, when you have looked around
And kitchen shears cannot be found,

I'd say, with just a trace of chiding,
They're not misplaced, poor things—they're hiding.

MIND OVER MATTRESS

Women make their minds (or heads) up
About the way they make their beds up:
First this then that side, back and forth,
From east to west and south to north,
They pull them tight, all tense and wary,
Then fluff them, puff them, make them airy.
At last, and with a final patting
That smooths both brain and cotton batting,
And with a sort of tuck and nipping
That's meant to hold and keep from slipping,
The bed or mind is tidied neatly—
Made up until it's changed completely.

WELL DEFINED

"To husband," says the dictionary,
Means to save, which I am very
Glad to know, but on my life,
It doesn't tell me what's "to wife."
And yet I didn't, I confess,
Look very hard—for I can guess.

CAPACITY CROWD

I love you from the bottom of my heart.
(Two other girls are in the upper part.)

HOME PLATE

Today my wife was at a luncheon
Where there was much to sip and munch on,
Where plates were piled up high and tasty
With stuff that makes a woman waisty,
Where, though there were around the fringes
Some guilty feelings, conscience twinges,
Dessert with fluffy whipped-cream topping
Was shoveled in without much stopping.

How do I know? Not on account of
My wife describing the amount of
Good food she knifed and forked from view
Between the hours of twelve and two.
Oh no, the reason in all fairness
For my suspicion, my awareness,
Is that, though I am starved tonight,
We're eating light.

HAIR LINES

A hairdresser, formerly a chemistry teacher, says that because hair is 97 percent protein, it should be fed protein.
He advises skim milk for setting hair, club soda for tinting,
salt in the shampoo for oily hair, and salad dressing for a
conditioner.—*News item.*

What the hair, it seems, is needing
Is less of care and more of feeding.
Those listless locks, those brittle bangs
Are doubtless feeling hunger pangs.

Although each hair is round, I'd say
Square meals are needed, three a day,
For hair, like anyone, must sup
To keep its protein content up.

It's not the beauty parlor where
You ladies need to take your hair.
No, it's the kitchen, nothing greater,
With head inside refrigerator.

CUTTING REMARKS

My wife uses scissors with reckless abandon.
It's scissors, I think, she has always her hand on.
She clips and she snips and she whicks and she
    whacks
Items out of the paper. I've not read the backs.
In front is a pattern, a bridge hand, a puzzle,
A recipe, maybe, for punch we can guzzle.
And what's on the back, that I never shall see?
Just something that's very important to me.
Indeed I'd save time, and I'll do it some day,
If I threw all the rest of the paper away—
So cunning her hand, with its cuttings and rippings,
I should read, for the news, just the backs of her
    clippings.

AFTER A FASHION

Consider, please, the fashion show
To which all shapes of ladies go,
The fat, the thin, the tall, the dumpy,
The scrawny, stringy, bony, bumpy.
They look at dresses svelte and rich
And in the latest fashion, which
Their husbands, I am sure, would buy
Without the batting of an eye
And lug straight home and help to pin them
If wives looked like the models in them.

NO COMPARISON

As I look at my wife,
  I regretfully see
She's not quite as young
  As I used to be.

ON MY WORD

A word to the wives is sufficient, I guess,
If it's Yes.

ROUGHING IT

We've left our kitchen, bright with chrome,
We've left our modern, cozy home,
We've left our plumbing, left our lights,
Left innersprings we slept on nights,
To cook in smoky, savage style
And carry water half a mile
And fill a rather chilly basin
To wash our grimy hands and face in
And lie upon the lumpy loam
And dream (if we can sleep) of home
And plumbing and electric lights
And innersprings we slept on nights.

ROOM SERVICE

When you are ill, my dear, I carry
Your breakfast on a tray.
I fluff your pillow up and tarry
With cheering things to say.

I put a robe around your shoulder,
I raise the window shade.
I warm your coffee when it's colder
And serve you like a maid.

When you are ill, I do your bidding—
You've but to ring a bell.
Some day I plan, my sweet (no kidding),
To do it when you're well.

ELECTED

One thing I think about a lot
Is how I got the wife I got,
And why, of all the men she knew,
I was the one and only who
Was singled out (culled out, perhaps)
From all the other likely chaps.

I doubt that I shall ever know
The reason why, but it is so,
And that's enough for any man,
Enough, at least, to give me an
Extremely high opinion of
Myself—for which my thanks, my dove.

About the Author

Richard Armour is one of the most widely read writers of humor and satire in America today. He has contributed thousands of articles and poems to more than two hundred magazines in the United States and England, and this is his thirty-seventh book.

His books include such satires of history and literature as *It All Started with Columbus, It All Started with Europa, American Lit Relit, Punctured Poems, Twisted Tales from Shakespeare,* and *The Classics Reclassified,* to mention only a few of the works that are the special favorites of high school and college students. Then there are his collections of light verse, such as *Light Armour, Nights with Armour,* and *The Medical Muse.* And there are those popular books on varied subjects: *Through Darkest Adolescence, Golf Is a Four-Letter Word, Our Presidents,* and *Going Around in Academic Circles.* He has also written several highly praised books for children, the latest being *A Dozen Dinosaurs* and *Odd Old Mammals.* Until the present book, his most autobiographical work was *Drug Store Days,* about his boyhood in the prescription room.

Though his books for many years have been in the field of satire, with sense always lurking beneath the nonsense, Richard Armour began as a serious scholar. A graduate of Pomona College and a Ph.D. from Harvard, he has written books of biography and literary criticism and has taught at a number of colleges and universities. Popular with students, he has lectured or been guest-in-residence on over two hundred campuses in various parts of the country. He has also lectured in both Europe and Asia as an American Specialist for the State Department.

Richard Armour served in the Army in both World War II and the Korean War, rising to the rank of colonel, and his *It All Started with Stones and Clubs* is at once a Swiftian satire and a condensed history of war and weaponry. A physical fitness buff, he swims, runs, lifts weights, and tires out those who watch him. Despite what he wrote about them in *Through Darkest Adolescence,* his son and daughter eventually grew up to be normal adults. He and his wife live in Claremont, California.